Contents

Foreword

by Lord Bullock

In 1972 I was asked by the Secretary of State for Education to chair a Committee of Inquiry 'to consider in relation to schools: all aspects of teaching the use of English, including reading, writing and speech; how present practice might be improved and the role that initial and in-service training might play; and to what extent monitoring the general level of attainment in these skills can be introduced and improved'.

In presenting our Report, *A language for life,** we expressed our reluctance to single out special recommendations because we were 'opposed from the outset to the idea that reading and the use of English can be improved in any simple way'. 'The solution,' we suggested, 'does not lie in a few administrative strokes, nor in the adoption of one set of teaching methods to the exclusion of another. Improvement will come about only from a thorough understanding of the many complexities, and from action on a broad front.'

The Committee, of course, paid considerable attention to broadcasting as a very important resource for reading and language development in schools, but – apart from noting the opportunities offered by Open University degree and post-experience courses – we were not able to pursue the wider question of the contribution which broadcasting might make to the in-service training of teachers. I am very glad, therefore, to learn of the plans BBC Radio has made, through its Further Education department, to offer two consecutive short courses in 1976 and in 1977 for those already concerned in schools with *Teaching young readers.*

This handbook accompanies the first of these two courses, designed for teachers in infant and junior schools (the second, in a year's time, will be for teachers in middle and secondary schools). I am reassured to see that it does not seek to provide specific answers to any of the

problems posed. Quite rightly, in my opinion, it prefers to suggest ways of approaching these problems: through the diagnosis of needs; through the selection of appropriate methods and resources for particular children; through the choice and organisation of different class activities for specific purposes; through the evaluation of work done in the classroom; and, above all, through the development of an overall policy for language education in the school. Beyond that, the authors recognise clearly that the teacher is often faced with thirty or more children in her class, with different backgrounds, different needs and abilities, and, though they may be roughly the same age, at different stages of personal development. And all of them are making their various demands on her, often at the same time.

I hope that the suggestions put forward in this handbook, taken in conjunction with the associated radio broadcasts, will help the individual teacher – and the school of which she is part – to cope more effectively with all these demands. If so, the course will have made a valuable contribution to the improvement of English language learning among the young. I am confident that it can.

Bullock

* HMSO 1975

Introduction

There are scores of books on the teaching of reading – so why produce another one? This book and the series of radio programmes it accompanies concentrate not on specific approaches or methods, but on practical classroom organisation. This book offers ways of exploring problems of school and classroom management as a means of helping you – the individual teacher – exploit the opportunities and resources available to you and maximise your own and your children's capabilities. It is relatively easy to plan and carry through a programme of activities designed to teach one particular child to read. Most teachers have thirty or more children in their class and the task is correspondingly more difficult. The problem is fundamentally one of organisation and this is the central theme of *Teaching young readers*.

The authors of this book have not produced a step-by-step guide to organising reading activities in the classroom – it would be foolhardy to try since all schools, all teachers and all children are different. It is for you – the individual teacher to find and develop the style of organisation that best suits you and the needs of your children and produces results. We hope that this book will provide you with the opportunity and the means to do just that.

Part 1 What is reading all about?

by Joan Dean, Chief Inspector for Surrey

John Smith left school at sixteen with five O levels and went to work in the central offices of a large county authority. Now, after ten years, and experience in several departments, he is working in a fairly senior post in the Education Department. His ability to do this job depends very substantially on his ability to read and write, and it is rare for him to pass an hour in the office without using these skills.

He also uses reading and writing a great deal in his spare time. He has always been an avid reader and enjoys a wide variety of fiction and non-fiction books. He takes and reads several periodicals. He is the secretary of his local gardening club and does a good deal of correspondence and searches through catalogues for them. He writes most of the family letters and keeps a diary for long spells.

For John Smith, reading is a source of income, information and pleasure, and it plays a very important part in his life.

Linda Jones is a young housewife with one child who has just started school and a three-year-old. She was not very successful at school and took a long time to learn to read. Even now she does not read much for pleasure, although she enjoys bits of the Sunday paper and some women's magazines. She is nevertheless obliged to read such things as recipes and instructions on how to do things, letters from her child's school, information about cheap offers at the supermarket and other day to day bits of information. She also finds herself pressured to write letters when her child is absent from school and now that she lives a long way from her own family, she needs to write to them and read what they write to her.

Why do we need to read?

Most people come somewhere between John Smith and Linda Jones, between those who read and write continually and those who do it as little as possible. The majority read for pleasure at some time or other and scan a newspaper. Most people find the need to follow written instructions occasionally, to discover how to work a petrol pump or the machine at the launderette. Most people find a need to read tax forms, rate demands, bills, advertising literature, labels on bottles of medicines, letters from school, election addresses and so on. Most people also find they need to write from time to time, however hesitantly and reluctantly.

The adult literacy campaign has shown us the problems of being illiterate in a literate world. All the developments in other media have simply served to emphasise the need for a high degree of skill because they have served to make our lives more complex and sophisticated.

Reading is not only a necessary skill for everyday living. It can also enlarge your view of the world by seeing it through the eyes of others. These may be people whom you have never met, who may even be long dead. It is true that radio and television also do this effectively, but you have only to read the book of a story you have watched to realise how much the written text differs from the television play. The picture may fill out your mental picture of how a character looks, but it can never express what he is thinking in the way the book can. Nor can you vary the speed of the film or broadcast according to your own rate of absorption. You can with a book. You can wander away from a book and come back without missing anything. You can skip and choose the bits you want to read and forget the rest. You can also select the book you want when you want it.

7

One further very important function of books and stories which is particularly true for children and young people, which is only partly met by television, is that they can help our growing. We all need to be able to see our own experience alongside that of others so that we can generalise and learn from it. We need to digest and come to terms with what happens to us, sometimes by escaping into fantasy for a while, sometimes by reading about the way other people cope with similar experiences. Children growing up have a particular need too for reading and learning about what happens next – what it is like to be a ten-year-old or a fourteen-year-old, so that they can prepare for their own growing.

Reading also provides us with an endless source of information and here again you can select what you happen to want – if you can find it. You can discover how to do something, make something, get somewhere. You can find out how things happen and why they happen. You can develop your understanding of other people and the world around us through reading, and you can read about what is happening outside your own locality. Radio and television do some of these things for us and sometimes do them more effectively, but the book and the newspaper still remain important sources of pleasure and information.

You need a variety of reading and writing skills

Each of these uses of reading requires a different range of skills. The fluent reader is taking meaning directly from marks on paper whatever the material, but if you are reading a detective story you may be running your eyes quickly over the page, leaving out the bits which you don't think are relevant. If you are reading a psychology book you will probably read much more slowly. If you read

poetry you may be wanting to say the words to yourself and listen to their sounds as well as thinking about their meaning. You look differently at a newspaper from the way you are looking at this book, differently at instructions from the way you look at stories. You need to be able to use these skills flexibly as you require them.

There are also a number of skills involved in using the printed word. You must be able to find what you need not only within a library but also within a text. You need not only to understand what is written but also to be able to make judgements about a text. You need to be able to assess what the writer says in the light of your own experience, your know-ledge of his experience and of statements by other writers. You therefore need skills in comparing texts and assessing them. You also need to be able to 'read' what *isn't* written in a text. Every piece of writing makes assumptions about the reader and implies rather than says some things, and you need skill in discovering what is implied rather than said. There are also very varied skills involved in writing. You need the skills of handwriting and spelling and the ability to use the conventions of written language appropriately. You also need to be able to match the language to the reader and to select appropriate forms of writing for different purposes, so that writing becomes a flexible tool of effective communication.

What are we doing when we read?

Reading is a complex process. The fluent reader looks at a series of marks on paper which immediately call up images of meaning. The reader who isn't yet fluent goes through an intermediate process. He looks at the marks and first matches them with a store of images of sounds of words, and then with

1 The child looks at the word;
2 breaks it up and matches the symbols with
images in her mind;
3 puts the sounds together and says the word;
4 matches the word with an image of its meaning.

images of meaning. At an earlier stage still he may need to build the words from images of their component sounds before starting on the process leading to meaning.

Your ability to understand what a writer is saying depends upon how successfully you can match the words he is using with images from your own experience. It is very easy to misunderstand something because the experience you bring to it differs from that of the writer.

Children have much shorter experience than adults and the store of images of experience a child may have is going to depend very much on the way in which adults have helped him to focus on experiences by drawing attention to certain things and by talking about them. Language must be part of the initial experience. As the child's experience grows, so he needs more language to talk about it. He will also fill out the images he brings to his existing language. A child just learning to talk may look at a flower and the adult with him may say something like 'daisy' and the child may repeat it. He may

then go on to point out other flowers and say *daisy*, but gradually his experience of flowers will develop and he will know that *daisy* is one of many flower names.

It is therefore a very important aspect of learning to provide a great deal of first-hand experience and the language both spoken and written, which goes with it.

A child needs a concept of what people are doing when they read

Learning to read involves acquiring some important concepts. The first of these is an understanding of what people are actually doing when they read. A child may see his parents scan a newspaper, read letters, follow instructions and signs or get buried in a book. These activities may seem puzzling at first, especially if his parents don't read more than they can help. From his point of view he sees Mum or Dad looking at a lot of marks on paper and sometimes apparently drawing information of some kind from them. If his parents read to him, he sees this process more

9

clearly at work, but he may still think the adult is making up a story round the pictures.

Children from literate homes usually get the idea of what reading is about long before they start school and by five they will probably recognize quite a number of words and be trying to write for themselves. They have often been doing 'pretend' writing for quite a time. Other children may be only just grasping the concept of reading and a few will not have grasped it at all.

Recognising words and letters

Once the initial concept of reading has been established, most children will begin to recognise words which have meaning for them. Their own names come high on this list, together with words which have emotional content and stir up feelings like *ice-cream* and *chocolate* and *mummy*. They will pick up and recognise some words from things around the house – like *Hoover*, *cornflakes* and so on, though these may be in trade mark versions rather than straightforward printing. At this stage the child is generally recognising the word by its whole shape and is probably using bits of detail to distinguish it from other words. These may not always be relevant details, and there is another important set of concepts here. Each letter has a wide variety of forms.

E can be: eEℯℰ𝓔e

T can be: tTt𝒯tt

to show but a few. *a* and *g* are particularly familiar to teachers of young children as being letters whose variety of form can cause confusion. Some letters are the same as others but the other way round – *p*, *d* and *b* for example, and *n* and *u*. This is a contradiction of the child's previous experience.

At quite an early stage in his life he will learn that an object looks different when you see it from a different angle. A thing that looks like this

can look like this

or like this

but it is still the same cup. At school he learns that

are all triangles and the way up and the way round they are doesn't matter. But in writing the way up and the way round do matter and letters like *a* and *d* and *n* and *h*, though they are the same way up and the same way round, are very little different from each other to a non reader.

The child's task is therefore to sort out which bits of letters tell you what they are, and to discover which way round different letters have to be. This is of particular importance as the child starts to write and he is very dependent on his teacher to draw attention to what is significant in each letter –

what is it that is constant about *e* for example, which helps us to recognise it whatever its form? It is also part of the word recognition process. What is it that tells us that *hand* is a different word from *nana*? The differences in detail are small but significant.

In other situations much larger differences appear not to matter. *Boat* for example, is the same as *BOAT* or *boat*. It can all be very confusing for a time if the teacher is not aware that such confusion can arise.

Gradually a child starts to build a store of images of words and letters in his mind and to associate these with meaning of some kind, so that when he sees a word written it conjures up first an image of the sound of the word itself and then images of the reality it represents

Structure and content

Some words provide images more easily than others, because they are content words like *table, house* or *car*. Other kinds of words can be more difficult to deal with. These are the structure words, many of which express relationships between things – relationships of time and place and causality like *over, because, then* and so on. These too are related to experience, but the teacher needs to work harder to be sure that the child understands. It isn't so much a matter of adding to a child's vocabulary, as a matter of adding to the ideas he can express. Can he use language to talk about what happened yesterday and what will happen tomorrow? Can he speculate on what would happen if . . .? Has he words for comparing things? Does he use pronouns properly? Has he grasped the ways we usually make plurals so that he can have a sensible shot at giving you the plurals of words that are new to him. Can he talk about why something happened? How far has he got towards using complex sentences in talking

and later in writing? Does he appear to understand these things when others use them? How do you know?

Written and spoken language

Most teachers try to work on from the recognition of individual words and phrases often by writing at the child's dictation a phrase or sentence, perhaps about a picture or model. She might, for example, write *John's mummy is going shopping*, by his picture or *Sally made this house* by a model. This approach, properly used, helps to bridge the gap between spoken and written language.

It is not always sufficiently recognised how big the gap is between a child's speech and his early reading material. Written language differs from spoken language in many ways. Spoken language uses inflection as part of meaning. Thus, even a sentence as simple as *John hit Janet* can be said with emphasis on any of the three words or none of them. *John hit Janet* differs in meaning from *John hit Janet* and *John hit Janet* and *John hit Janet*.

These differences can only be shown in writing by underlining or italic type, and this is the reason for the various extra marks we use in writing. The same sentence can also read *John hit Janet?* and *John hit Janet!* and *John, hit Janet!* We also use language slightly differently in writing. We rarely speak tidy sentences, for example, but we try to write that way. Some words like *replied* are more frequent in writing than in speech. Writing also tends to be a bit more formal than speech.

The child starting to write has all this to learn, but he first needs to establish the idea that what he can say, he can write and that if he passes this to someone else, they will be able to read it and know what he said, even if they didn't hear him say it. The most obvious way to help a child understand the basic idea of communication through reading and writing is to use the child's own language. The scheme *Breakthrough to literacy* (see part 4, page 118) extends the idea so that children use their own language not only to copy or trace over what the teacher has written, but also as a store of individual words to build new sentences. This has the advantage of helping them reinforce their knowledge of the words they use in speaking. It also has the advantage of showing that the same words can be arranged in different ways and that word order matters. It is not necessary to use *Breakthrough* to use this technique, however.

Learning to write goes alongside learning to read for most children. It must include at an early stage some teaching in how to form letters, so that children do not build up habits of letter formation which will slow them up later. A child will need to learn to copy, at first going over his teacher's writing, then copying under it, before going on to copy from work cards and later from the board, which can be much more difficult for some children. As soon as he has enough words to build sentences he needs to use them in as many ways as possible, so that he is constantly needing to recognise them and remember them afresh.

Word building and decoding

Once a child has acquired a reasonable sight vocabulary, he needs to develop word building and decoding skills. There are really four separate skills here. He needs first to be able to hear sounds in words. Then he needs to be able to match sound and symbol. The next stage is to blend symbols together to make words and conversely, to be able to break down the words he meets so that he can discover what they say. Blending in particular is a skill peculiar to reading and many children have some difficulty in acquiring it.

It is not as simple a matter as it sometimes seems. In the first place it is extremely difficult

---

Important words in learning to read   MURRAY/MCNALLY

a and he I in is it of that the to was all as at be but are for had have him his not on one said so they we with you about an back been before big by call came can come could did do down first from get go has her here if into just like little look made make more me much must my no new now off old only or our other out over right see she some their them then there this two up want well went were what when where which who will your

The hundred next most used words (nouns in italics)

after again always am another any ask away bad because best *bird* black blue *boy* bring *day dog* don't eat every far fast *father* fell find five fly four found gave *girl* give going good got green *hand head* help *home house* how jump keep know last left let live long *man* many may *men mother* Mr. never next once open own play put ran read red *room* round run sat saw say *school* should sing sit soon stop take tell than these *thing* think three *time* too *tree* under us very walk white why wish work would *year* to pronounce some sounds without adding an extra vowel. A sound, like *d*, for example, inevitably becomes *d–er*, however carefully you say it, so that in an extreme situation a child can go through the process of saying *a–er n–er d–er* and conclude that it makes the word *Canada*. You can partly overcome this by teaching consonant and vowel together whenever possible *ta* or *ti* rather than *t–i* or *t-a* or by using the Stott 'half moons' (see below) which help to convey the feeling of blending by putting the pieces together, but it is a problem to be watched for.

Blending also depends to some extent on a child's ability to hear sounds in his head and hold them long enough to work through a sequence and make up a word. Children with poor visual or auditory memory may find this difficult. Getting sounds written in the order you hear them or said in the order you see them also poses problems for some children.

A few children acquire phonic skills alongside word recognition skills without much help. Others need careful teaching and lots of practice. It is not enough merely to teach single sounds; children also need to learn the full range of blends and digraphs and while there are many ways of making this learning interesting and challenging, it is unlikely that the majority will acquire it without help.

Reading must have a purpose

While children are acquiring phonic skills, the teacher needs to do a good deal to keep fresh in their minds the idea that reading is an enjoyable activity, that it provides all kinds of interesting and useful information and that learning phonics is a means of achieving independence and autonomy. It is also valuable and necessary to provide a great deal of practice in recognising words within the child's competence to build. Word recognition needs to come before, alongside and after phonic learning, so that the child recognises words

Phonic knowledge Level 2

Spelling (group)

The teacher is interested in the child's knowledge of the rules governing the underlined portions of the words. She should ask him to spell the following words, or words of similar construction, to see if he knows how to transcribe the sounds given. Mark the child's satisfactory responses on the checklist. The blank spaces will indicate the rules needing extended practice, experience or instruction.

1 Digraphs

ship	what	quip
sh- ☐	wh- ☐	qu– ☐

2 Blends

blot brig scot	clap crack smut	flap drip snap	glen from spot	plan gran stop	slip pram swim	twit trap
bl– ☐ br– ☐ sc– ☐	cl– ☐ cr– ☐ sm– ☐	fl– ☐ dr– ☐ sn– ☐	gl– ☐ fr– ☐ sp– ☐	pl– ☐ gr– ☐ st– ☐	sl– ☐ pr– ☐ sw– ☐	tw– ☐ tr– ☐

3 Ending blends

duck	act	left	lamp	end	sing	went
-ck ☐	-ct ☐	–ft ☐	—mp ☐	-nd ☐	-ng ☐	-nt ☐

immediately whenever possible and uses word building skills as a prop when necessary.

Once a child can read a little, we need to help him use this skill. Even half a dozen words may be enough to tell him how to do something if they are carefully chosen. For example, a card on *shape* might say *Find 4 round things. Draw them. Write '4 round things'*. This uses six words and the figure 4. Similar messages are easy to devise. The skilled teacher can find all kinds of situations to get across the idea that the written and printed word is a medium for ideas and communication and not an end in itself.

She will use writing to tell children what to do or to show where things are kept or how they may be used. She will encourage children to put their own ideas in writing for others to read. She will take any opportunity which offers of getting children to write to the head or other teachers, to their parents or other children, perhaps inviting them to come to see something they have done or telling them about something which has happened.

4 Vowel changes: additional e or second vowel (*Where there are alternative spellings possible the teacher should ask the child if he knows the alternatives.)

	game		eve		home		duke		line		lied	
	mail*		meat*		boat		due		high		by*	
	pay		peep		poet				wild			

a–e		e–e		o–e		u–e		i–e		ie	
ai		ea		oa		ue		igh		y	
ay		ee		oe				il			

5 Addition of r

| | hair* | | far | | care | | hear* | | for | |
| | her | | fir* | | fire | | here | | tore* | |

| –air | | –ar | | –are | | –ear | | –or | |
| –er | | –ir | | –ire | | | | –ore | |

6 Other changes

| | read | | Paul | | boil | | book | | out | |
| | law | | few | | cow | | moon | | boy | |

| ea | | au | | oi | | oo | | ou | |
| aw | | ew | | ow | | oo | | oy | |

Written language should also be purposeful and should develop out of many classroom activities and whenever possible should be used for communication – even to the extent of teacher and child and child and child writing to each other rather than speaking on some occasions.

For example, with a class where most children can write reasonably well, it can be useful to insist for a short period, perhaps an hour or so, that all the children in one group ask any questions they wish to ask the teacher or others in the group by writing them down. Answers will also be given in writing.

For example, a child might write,

I've lost my red crayon.

The teacher might reply,

Get another one from the cupboard.

Another child might write,

I've finished my story. Can I read it to you?

And the teacher might reply,

I'll hear you next. Read your book for a minute.

15

This needs to be regarded as a bit of fun to be indulged in for a short time. It tends to be time consuming but stresses very well the communication aspect of writing.

It can also be useful to extend the Christmas letter box and encourage everyone to write and reply to letters for a time.

Developing further skills

As fluency develops, further skills in reading and writing can also be developed. Children need to learn to find their way around books, using contents pages and indexes. They need to learn to skim a page for information and compare what different books say. They can learn to use written instructions and perhaps to write them for others. They also need to develop the rather different kinds of skills needed for reading maps, diagrams and plans, and for reading mathematical symbols and music. Adult skill in reading and writing requires an appreciation of what is an appropriate use of reading skill for a given purpose. The fluent adult reader should be able to decide whether a text is for skimming through or for careful reading or for reading in whatever way seems enjoyable and select skills which seem to him to meet his purpose in reading.

These more advanced skills start to develop quite early for many children and you need to work to help them to establish habits which will support the range of reading skills they will need later, since nearly all these habits are established early and are difficult to change later.

A fluent reader takes meaning from the page much faster than he could say the words. Many people never reach this stage and find it difficult to improve their skills because of the habits they established as children. In particular some people read slowly because they use inefficient eye movements.

Children who are reaching this stage also need to know that when we read, we fix our eyes on points in the line of print and take in what is on each side of the point we have fixed on. The slow reader often fixes his eyes at the end of the line and thus can only take in what is on one side of the point he has fixed on. With help, a child can easily change this habit at the primary school stage. It is much more difficult to change later. Some children improve their reading skill simply by knowing that fluent readers do not always say the words they read and trying to match skill to purpose. The way written language develops tends to reflect the development of the child's thinking. At first sentences will be short and contain a single idea. They will gradually come to be linked with *ands* and eventually become more complex with one part of a sentence dependent on another. Although this development cannot be forced, it is to some extent affected by the models children are offered, and development may follow the introduction by the teacher of more complex and varied sentence forms.

Story writing usually gives rise to a fairly substantial development in language use and it is valuable for some time at least to allow children to write stories of whatever length they wish. Once real fluency has been obtained, it may be worth discussing ways of saying things briefly.

As writing develops it becomes increasingly important for children to write for varied purposes and varied audiences. Although it is inevitable that much is written for the teacher, there is an artificiality about this which means that many children do not learn the difference in writing for different readers and different purposes. Every possible opportunity is needed to write for real purposes and for different readers and able nine-year-olds are well able

Below: factual writing from first-hand experience.

we made Some Canoes in the garage. You
need glue, screws and nails. You have bits
shaped like a V you Stick them on the
Top then you put the Sides on with tacs
and glue then you Sand Paper them
then you put some other V blocks
In then we put the varnish you have
to put 3 coats on it. You have
to put Some thing red or Yellow on
the back. When You go Travelling. our
first test out was successful Went
down to Sonning Lock there we put them in.
we Went round the Island twice.

to produce writing which is appropriate for a given purpose, although the skills involved and the ability to make judgements about this will develop further at a later stage.

Learning to read is not a tidy process. The Bullock Report, *A language for life*, says 'Language competence grows incrementally, through an interaction of writing, talk, reading and experience'. Everything that happens during the child's day can contribute to the development of competence in the use of language but he is dependent on the adults about him for many important aspects of this development. The teacher who is clear about what is involved in learning to read and write will use the opportunities which arise in the day to day work of the classroom to further each child's progress. She will also go further and see that the right opportunities arise at the right time for individual children. This is not simply a matter of sitting a child or a group of children down to teach them something specific, although there is an important place for this. It also involves seeking ways of harnessing the will and power to learn which is in each child.

What goals do you have in your language teaching? Compare them with those in the next section.

Part 2   Organising language work

by Joan Dean

What are we trying to do?

The first section of this book sets out the goals of language education in terms of the skills needed in adult life. Every school and every teacher needs to consider these goals and to provide a language programme which will lead children towards them. This programme needs to be set down in writing. It should cover all aspects of language work and should set out the school's aims and philosophy clearly. It should be sufficiently short for teachers to know it well, but sufficiently comprehensive to cover all the work they may want to do. It might be expected to cover the following:–

● The development of the ability to use speech and writing to communicate simple needs, factual information, ideas, possibilities, feelings and emotions, clearly, lucidly and appropriately, including the ability to:–

(a) speak adequately and competently in a range of social situations;

(b) write appropriately for a variety of purposes and in a variety of forms;

(c) write clearly and arrange work well, use the conventions of written language and spell at an appropriate level.

● The development of the ability to understand and use the spoken, written and printed communication of others including the ability to:–

(a) listen to, understand and respond appropriately to the words of others;

(b) read for a variety of purposes in a variety of ways.

● The development of ideas and knowledge about language as well as skill in using it, including the development of:–

(a) appropriate vocabulary;

(b) an interest in words, their history and derivation;

(c) an appreciation of the idea that people use language differently according to their background and according to the situation.

● The development of attitudes leading to confidence, enjoyment of books and enthusiasm for reading and writing and to the ability to be properly critical and self-critical.

This outline will need a good deal of filling in. There will be a range of skills to be acquired in each area. Spoken language will include such things as work on developing language to recount experience, explain, give directions, teach, greet people, introduce them, entertain them, find things out from them, speak for various purposes to various kinds of audience and in various situations. Listening may involve the development of a number of kinds of discrimination and comprehension skills, including the ability to make inferences about a speaker from the way he speaks as well as understanding and evaluating what he says.

Reading development will need very full coverage and must include the range of pre-reading skills, the development of word recognition and phonic skills, through to the skills of reading for information and pleasure, using books to find out, comparing accounts, understanding what is read and developing skill in making inferences from it. A few children between the ages of 4 and 9 will also begin to develop the ability to read in different ways according to their purpose in reading and will have started to take information from the printed word faster than they can say the words and this should be included in the programme for those who progress to this stage quickly.

Written language will start with the

development of copying skills of various kinds and will include letter formation and the development of handwriting but will be mainly concerned with the build up of the child's ability to express himself in writing. The programme should include work on the development of different forms of writing stemming from different experiences – story writing, personal imaginative writing, poetry, factual writing, writing of instructions and directions, and so on. Opportunities for this kind of writing will come up in all aspects of work and we need to use the experiences to develop language skills as well as skills and knowledge in other work.

Children also gradually develop a sense of writing for a readership if their writing is frequently for a real purpose. The oldest children in this group are often able to distinguish between the way they may write for their teacher and the way they may write for other adults or other children.

Part of all this development will be increasing skill in using language in more complex ways. The programme will need to consider the degree to which children have learned to use the past and future in talking, their skill in using pronouns, plurals, prepositions and the way the gradually become able to use more complex sentences to express different ideas.

Does your school have a language programme? If it doesn't do you know why? Is it really necessary? In what form should a language programme be set out? What ought it to contain?

If your school does have a language programme how does it compare with the outline given on page 18? What use do you make of it?

There are many possible ways of setting out a language programme and there is certainly a need for setting out some of the theory behind it and making some comment on its relationship to what is known about language development in children. One fairly simple way of going on from there is to list a series of actual pieces of behaviour which embody the skills you want children to acquire. For example a reading programme might start with *matches shapes* and go on to statements like *reads own name, reads 100 key words* (or the word load in the books of the reading schemes used), *recognises/writes single consonants, etc.*

Write down the things you want your children to be able to do under the following headings. Each section has been started for you:

Pre-reading skills
Matches shapes
Matches letters
. . . .
. . . .

Word recognition skills
Recognises own name
Recognises 100 key words
. . . .
. . . .
. . . .

Phonic skills
Hears sounds in words
Can play 'I spy' with sounds
Matches sounds and symbols
. . . .
. . . .

Speaking
Speaks clearly
Uses past tense
Uses future tense

Uses prepositions
Talks about first-hand experience

. . . .

. . . .

Listening
Listens to stories and answers questions

. . . .

. . . .

Writing
Traces over teacher's writing
Copies teacher's writing

. . . .

. . . .

A list like this can be built up by a staff group and can then be used as a record for each child. It has the advantage of recording the kind of information about each child that every teacher needs to know. It also enables every teacher to become really familiar with the language programme.

This kind of exercise does not do the whole job, however. There are many important aspects of language work which cannot easily be reduced to a piece of behaviour which you need to be looking for. The development of attitudes, for example, is of very considerable importance and assessment of what is happening to a particular child is the result of accumulating many small pieces of evidence over a long period. Imaginative and creative ability too is largely a matter of subjective judgement.

Although this kind of development cannot be listed in terms of individual pieces of behaviour, there is much to be said for having a written guide to observation or checklist, like the one shown opposite, particularly for the inexperienced teacher. When children first come to school, for example, it is useful to note how a child settles in, how he responds to his teacher

and to other children. Does he persist at a task? draw at an appropriate level? and so on. Later we may want to note interest in books, enthusiasm for particular kinds of activity, growing confidence and many other things.

Teachers are often unhappy about checklists because they feel that important aspects of work have to be omitted. What aspects of language work are difficult to put as part of a checklist? What are the clues by which we judge our success in these aspects of work?

Guides to observation are no more than guides, however. The teacher's ability to observe children is crucial and is best developed by practice and by observing with other teachers and talking about what has been seen.

Not every head and staff choose to set out the language programme in this way. Many heads prefer a more general statement. And whether your school has a detailed language programme or not, you will need to identify your own objectives, preferably in writing, with many of them stated as pieces of behaviour. If you do this, you have a means of assessing your progress in helping children to achieve them. You also provide yourself with a useful checklist, which can serve as a framework for your organisation. The following suggestions may help you to do this.

● Look back at the information given about objectives at the beginning of this section on page 18. Note which areas concern the children you are teaching. Check whether the simplest and the most difficult areas you have noted will be right for your most and least able children.

● Set out as much of this as you can as statements of observed behaviour of individuals. Where this seems difficult, ask

ST. PETER'S C. OF E. SCHOOL, FARNHAM   LANGUAGE RECORD

Name ....   Date of birth ....

    Teacher's initials ....

SPOKEN LANGUAGE

A Speech

1 Articulates clearly

2 Uses prepositions correctly

3 Uses past and future tenses correctly [ ]   Has speech difficulty [ ]

B Use of speech

1 Talks about first hand experience   a) to teacher
    b) to a group

2 Delivers a simple message

3 Carries on a conversation

4 Talks about probabilities and possibilities

5 Tells a story

6 Talks about feelings and emotions

7 Can reason in language

8 Explains something to, or teaches someone else

9 Gives directions for finding way over known route

10 Answers telephone and takes message correctly

11 Shows visitor round school

12 Takes part in class or group discussion

13 Interviews and asks questions to find out

C Listening and recording

1 Listens to stories and can answer questions on their content

2 Listens and responds correctly to instructions and explanations

WRITING

A Handwriting and layout

1 Hand used

2 Holds pencil correctly

3 Copies from board

4 Can join letters

5 Can space out and present work well   a) with lines
    b) without lines

B Conventions

1 Usually gets letters in right order

2 Usually writes in sentences, using capitals and punctuation correctly

3 Punctuation

.	,	" "	;	'	?

C Use of writing

1 Writes news

2 Writes stories and other imaginative work

3 Writes to given title or outline

4 Distinguishes fact from fiction and writes one or other intentionally

5 Writes instructions for someone else

6 Reports factual information and first hand experience

7 Writes poetry

8 Writes letters giving address correctly

9 Makes notes from books

10 Makes notes from TV or Radio

11 Makes notes from interviews or discussions

12 Puts notes together to make coherent whole

13 Writes appropriately for a given purpose

READING

A Initial skills

(Read in conjunction with check list)

1 Knows at sight 100 most used words

2 Knows sounds (as on check list)

3 Blends sounds to build words

4 Uses knowledge of phonics to read new words

B Using books and writing

1 Uses alphabetical order

2 Uses indices and contents lists

3 Finds books needed for information

4 Finds material needed in text

5 Compares different accounts in different books

6 Works from written instructions

C Advanced skills

1 Can read aloud fluently with good expression

2 Can skim

3 Enjoys reading

4 Is aware of need to read in different ways for different purposes

yourself what clues there will be to tell you whether something is happening. What are the clues which tell a child's attitudes, for example?

● Make this statement positive, noting what a child can do. You will need to note what he can't do somewhere else.

This statement can now be used as a record for each child.

Organising language work — how shall we do it for the school?

Organisation is the way in which a school or an individual teacher translates theory into practice. You can have a marvellous theoretical understanding of the way children learn to read and splendid ideas, but if you can't plan so that children actually learn, you are not really much use to them as a teacher.

This fact is sometimes taken to mean that theory doesn't matter; that all we need to be concerned with is the practical work in the classroom. This is nearly as bad as assuming that only theory matters. When a school staff takes the view that it is a waste of time to work out together what children should learn and why and how they should learn it, what is happening is that everyone is relying on a set of assumptions which are never made explicit. The trouble is that the underlying assumptions of different teachers may in fact differ much more widely than they suppose. The children will be the losers because what one teacher does may not be reinforced by the next teacher. The most successful schools are those where the staff achieve something of a common vision and if this draws in parents to some extent as well, the children's learning is constantly reinforced.

Common vision doesn't happen overnight. It is the result of a good deal of thinking and talking on the part of teachers and an openness in their attitudes to each other, so that they help each other's thinking and development. It requires some clear thinking about overall aims and short and long term objectives.

These then need to be translated into an overall pattern of organisation for the school and into individual patterns of organisation in the classrooms and work spaces. These overall patterns need to be developed by teachers working together, although there is an important place for someone whose task is to lead and coordinate.

What aspects of the language programme need to be agreed by the whole staff? What aspects need to be coordinated on a school basis?

The school, like the teacher in the classroom, has to accept some factors in organisation over which it has little or no control. The staff and children work within parameters decided by the LEA. The school provides for a given neighbourhood and its organisation and the work it attempts will be affected by the population of the area. A school may organise differently in a mainly middle class suburb, from the way it might organise in a deprived inner city area or in a small village or a farming community. These are 'givens' and the school must come to terms with them.

Any individual school also starts with a given collection of teachers, each of whom brings skills and expertise of different kinds, different strengths and weaknesses and different styles. These are all factors which need to be taken into account in considering the overall organisation.

There are also factors for the school as well as for the teacher which are much more within the school's control. The materials available may be limited by capitation allowances, but schools can choose what they buy and how they use them. Time is finite, but there are many ways of planning its use. The staffing ratio is given, but the ways in which children can be grouped for learning are many and varied.

Each school therefore has important decisions to make about the way that learning is to be organised. Any organisation must fit the children and the teachers for whom it is designed and it must be sufficiently flexible to change to meet new needs as they arise. There are many good ways of organising and each form of organisation will have positive things to offer and some areas where it is less satisfactory. Every school and every teacher will be different.

Nevertheless, so far as language is concerned there are some *essentials*. Every school needs the kind of language programme, in writing, that was discussed at the beginning of this book on page 18.

If this programme is to work effectively, with each teacher contributing in her own style to a programme which adds up for each child, a good deal of talking and thinking needs to be done by everyone concerned. Having a written programme doesn't ensure continuity in approaches and demands on children.

What induction/training programme is needed for teachers new to the school as far as language work is concerned? What induction/training programme is needed for probationers and experienced teachers? How is this best provided?

The role of the coordinator

Every school needs to have someone responsible for coordinating language work, who draws together the thinking of the staff as a basis for the scheme, holds meetings to discuss approaches and ideas, oversees the distribution of books, equipment, and audio visual resources and develops systems for their use, watches the market for new ideas and new materials, helps teachers to evaluate their work and keep records, inducts new teachers and supports the inexperienced as well as doing many other things to foster language development.

In a very small school the head may wish to do this work, but once the staff numbers seven or eight, you need someone without too many other responsibilities, because if it is to be well done, it will require a great deal of work.

It is worth emphasising that in today's climate it is no longer a matter of the head or some other senior member of staff laying down firm rules for others to follow without question. This assumes a less than professional attitude on the part of teachers. If a school is really to make progress, many issues must be discussed and the patterns which emerge and are agreed should be patterns to which many have contributed, even though they may be drawn together and put on paper by one person.

Do you have a coordinator responsible for language work in your school? Do you think it important to have one and what should her responsibilities be?

The coordinator and language resources

The coordinator needs to be responsible for language materials and books, and in a very large school it may be necessary to have someone else working with her looking after the library. Many teachers feel happiest when they have acquired their own collection of reading materials within their own classrooms and once they achieved this, feel little need to borrow from others. This view has its advantages and certainly every teacher needs to be able to rely on having material she knows well easily to hand. The trouble about dealing with materials in this way is that there is no guarantee that materials will be well used – a piece of apparatus may remain in the cupboard in one room, even though it is exactly what the teacher at the other end of the school desperately needs.

The school needs some way of making much of what is in stock available to everyone, without running into the problems of an individual teacher never knowing whether she can have what she needs when she needs it, or the problem of things being returned with bits missing.

One way of dealing with this is to develop a coding system which is used by all the teachers. It would be possible, for example, for the whole staff to agree that all pre-reading material should be marked with circular spots, all word recognition materials with squares and all phonic material with triangles. Within these categories, different colours can be used for different sections of work. Different coloured squares in the word recognition section, for example, might designate material related to different stages of the main reading scheme. Different coloured triangles in the phonic section might show which materials dealt with single consonants, which with short vowels and so on.

If a system of this kind is used for all materials, teachers can borrow from each other or from a central collection, knowing what they are looking for. A useful way of starting this off is to get everyone to put all her

material out on tables in the hall and then to sort it all into categories such as those described earlier, perhaps pre-reading material, word recognition material, phonic material and so on. Each of these major sections can be given a symbol and sections within it can be given a colour. Each piece of material can then be listed under the sections and sub-sections, and its whereabouts in the school noted and the full list can be duplicated so that every teacher in the school has a copy. Everyone then knows exactly what is available around the school to help children to learn blending for example.

This exercise has the added advantage of showing up the major gaps, which tend to exist in every school. In an ideal situation there would be several pieces of material designed to help a child acquire each skill, so that the child who needed a great deal of help and repetition was not faced with the same material over and over again. Ideally there should be very varied material available to teach each skill – perhaps work sheets and cards, audio visual material of some kind, a game or two and some simple programmed learning material. This makes it possible for teachers to match material to children, as well as providing variety for slow learners.

Where such an exercise shows very substantial gaps, they need to be filled quickly. The quickest way to fill gaps is to make work sheets which can be duplicated. A group of teachers within a school or at a teachers' centre can discuss what they need and then each makes some work sheets, which can be available to everyone. There should, of course, be variety in materials eventually, but work sheets provide one of the quickest ways of getting enough material, and give time to build up more varied approaches.

Once all the material has been coded and

catalogued much of it can go back to the rooms of individual teachers and there can be agreement about borrowing. Probably the best arrangement to work towards is to see that every room has a basic stock of material designed to teach all the necessary skills, with a central collection or collections of further material which can be available as necessary.

The coordinator then has the task to see that all new material is coded and listed. She also needs to see that new members of staff are aware of the system and what is available to them.

If materials are to be shared and good use made of them, they must all be properly packaged with devices for easy checking where there are a number of pieces. They also need to be stored in such a way that it is easy for a teacher to find what she needs, both in the classroom and centrally. Suggestions about packaging are given elsewhere.

The central store of materials can be partly on shelves in cupboards, where expensive equipment is concerned and partly in filing cabinets or improvised filing. Shelves need to be fairly near together for a lot of material, because boxes stacked on top of each other tend to get untidy. Every container should be labelled clearly so that the label and coding shows when it is stacked. It is also useful when materials are on shelves to draw round the base of each object and label the space so that people return materials to their proper places.

Filing cabinets and improvised filing can be used for work sheets and some flat games and these too need proper labelling.

There should be a fair amount of tape/slide material available and this will need suitable storage. There may very often be books or work cards to go with these, so they may be best housed in a box altogether, with the slides in a plastic wallet with pockets. The present price of daylight viewers makes it possible to house one in each box.

Books are, of course, the major resource for reading and they too need careful organisation. There are now a good many lists available to help teachers to classify the reading levels of different books and this needs to be done for all the reading material, using a colour code which is known to every child and teacher. This should be a different code from the one suggested earlier on page 25 for materials but there could be common features. For example, the same sequence of colours might be used to represent the sequence of difficulty in both schemes.

The important thing about books is that they should be easily available when children need them. This means putting them in easily accessible places. It also means having an overall system which makes it possible to find what you need when you need it.

In some open plan schools it will be possible to have a book area serving a group of classes or a team. Some small schools will also have central book areas. These will make more books available to more children if the teachers can organise it so that they are really well used, but this organisation brings with it a need to organise the books carefully so that it is easy to keep them in order and to return them to the right places. It is important that someone is responsible for such an area and that ways of dealing with the books are agreed by all the teachers. With the younger children it is more important to arrange books according to codings which show levels of difficulty, but as children start to use books for information then some fairly simple subject grouping may be needed. Book areas today ought also to contain tapes and slides and pictures, organised in a similar way to the books.

The majority of schools will have most of their books in individual classrooms. It is still important in this situation to have an overall coding for difficulty so that children can, where necessary, have access to books in other classrooms. It is also important to have a sufficient range of books in each room – both in subject matter and difficulty. Where the overall book stock is small, it may be useful to have regular exchanges between classes.

Another important aspect of the provision of books is the way they are chosen. The coordinator needs to evolve ways in which a number of teachers give care and thought to what is bought for the school. This means studying the reviews, visiting libraries and bookshops and spending time considering what is available. Many local authorities have Children's Librarians who provide a great deal of help and advice for teachers, but this does not let the teachers themselves out of the important task of choosing books.

Many factors will enter into choice – vocabulary and language structures; print size and page layout; illustrations; topics and stories. Young children need good quality materials in all aspects of their school life and the books we give them must be good of their kind, well written and well illustrated as well as being of interest to children and at the right level. There should be discussion about choice of books among the staff of a school and encouragement to parents to be interested and to buy.

How are books chosen in your school? What criteria are used for choosing them?

Books need the right sort of housing and display. Most schools today are conscious of the need to create attitudes to books and reading by making attractive areas for them and enticing children in. Carpet and easy chairs, wallpaper and curtains to a book area make it homelike and start associations for reading. They are only useful, however, if the associations really are established and if the children really come to see books as enjoyable and exciting and interesting.

This is most likely to happen where the books themselves are well displayed with the covers showing. Small children choose books by their appearance to a much greater extent than older children or adults and we need to take this into account, and really show the books.

See page 72 for more about resource organisation, display and storage.

Coordinating the language of reading

Another important but neglected area in which the school programme needs coordination is in the language used to talk about reading. The way we talk about reading to children often seems so basic that the teacher does not feel it necessary to explain, and few schools at present coordinate this sufficiently. There is a good deal which children need to learn. The word *letter* for example, to the pre-school child, is the thing that the postman brings. The teacher uses the word to mean something different and this needs to be explained, along with words like *word, sentence, symbol* and so on.

Almost all schools and teachers use the following words in teaching reading:

word   *capital letter*
letter   *sentence*

Are you sure that your children understand them?

In teaching reading you need to talk about the following, but different teachers give them different names:

sound	*letter name*
symbol	*vowel*
small letters	*consonant*
(lower case)	*digraph*
silent e	*silent letter*
marker e	*plural*
magic e	

What do you call these?

When you teach handwriting you need words like:

first	*up/down*
last	*same/different*
beginning	*clockwise*
curved	*anti-clockwise*
straight	*left/right*

Do your children understand them?

You will also want to talk about punctuation and use these words

full stop	*speech marks*
comma	*apostrophe*
question mark	*inverted commas*
exclamation mark	

What do you call them?

It is worth remembering that children usually have little difficulty in learning naming words and it may therefore be as easy to use a word like *digraph* as to call a digraph a *two-letter sound* or something similar. Changing the name of something doesn't necessarily make the idea it expresses any easier.

Confusion may also arise because a child moves from one teacher to the next and finds that the new teacher uses different words to talk about reading. Perhaps his first teacher talked about *two-letter sounds* and his new teacher talks about *digraphs*. One teacher may talk about the *magic –e* and another may call it a *marker* and yet another the *silent –e*. Some reading schemes suggest terminology, but whatever words are used, they really should be agreed upon and used by everyone.

Coordinating record keeping and evaluation

A school needs not only a coordinated language programme. It also needs the kind of evaluation and record keeping system which watches carefully over the progress of each child. Each teacher will want to keep personal records of various kinds and will be evaluating her work as she goes along, but more is needed.

It is essential that each school keeps adequate records of the progress of individual children and that these are passed on from teacher to teacher. These need to be the working records of the teacher. When you start work with a new class, you may welcome a pen portrait of each child, but what you really need to know as a teacher is what he does and does not know, can and cannot yet do, the things that appear to work in teaching him and those which are less successful, the topics which he has covered individually or in a group and with what success, the books he has read and so on. You won't take all this information in at once for every child, but if it is set out in a fairly simple format which is the same for every child, you will take in enough to get started and you can then return to the record as you get to know the child.

It is also valuable for a staff to set out to make overall evaluations of their work from time to time. An increasing number of local authorities are monitoring progress in reading and this information can be very valuable. If your LEA is not testing all the children at some stage it may be worth doing this for yourself. This kind of exercise might conclude with some concentrated attention on the children who are reading well below their chronological age and some thought should also be given to those at the upper extremes. There will also be some children whose performance is well below what might be expected from them. All these groups of children need to be studied; their problems noted and programmes planned for them.

The head of a school or the coordinator also needs to look at the work of individual teachers, talk with them and help them in any way she can. It may also be useful to draw on the expertise of the local advisory service and the school psychological service in evaluating what is happening.

(See also page 82).

What records need to be kept on a school basis? How should a school evaluate language work?

Organising language work — how shall we do it in the classroom?

Every school and every teacher has to go on from formulating aims and objectives to putting them into action. Any school's ability to help children reach its goals is only as good as the organisation for learning that is set up, and the relationship of organisation and goals needs to be under constant review because in every organisation there are strengths and weaknesses.

Sometimes children learn what you want them to learn, but might have learnt more quickly and effectively in a different organisation. Sometimes a few children learn very well and others learn inadequately. In all organisations some children learn all sorts of things besides those you want them to learn. For example, in a situation where children have to wait for the teacher to tell them what to do next at each stage, the brightest children may learn to work slowly so that they don't spend time waiting to see you. You need to be constantly searching for the form of organisation which enables the maximum number of children to learn as effectively and fully as possible with the fewest disadvantages.

I have already said that some aspects of organisation are outside the control of the school. The LEA dictates the size of the school, the age groups it caters for, the staffing ratio and the allowances available.

Do you know the facts and figures that relate to your school?

Every school serves a particular neighbourhood and you have to work with those children and their parents. A school is stuck with the limitations of its buildings and each teacher with the limitations of her classroom. Individual teachers are also limited by the things agreed and arranged on a school basis, like the main reading scheme or the use of the hall, for example.

There are other aspects of organisation, like the grouping of children, the use of materials, equipment and space and the use of time which are much more within the control of the school and the individual teacher who can also vary teaching approaches and the grouping of children inside the classroom.

Given factors

Children

Parents and neighbourhood

The school staff

Buildings, equipment and materials

Variables

Learning activities

Teaching approaches

Grouping of children

Use of time
    space
    equipment
    materials

The given factors

You need to study the *givens* if you want to use the *variables* effectively.

The most important *given* is the children. They need continual study if you are to plan for their learning, taking into account the infinite variety of their backgrounds, experiences, interests and development. With this in mind, let's start by looking in some detail at six children and their individual learning needs.

The children: Doreen

Doreen is eight. She has an IQ of 128 but her reading quotient on the *Young test* is only 96. She is the elder of two girls, with a very bright and confident young sister in nursery school. Her mother is dour, tense and anxious.

Doreen is talkative, shows off a lot, is rather pushing and brash upon occasions, but on other occasions is very adult and entertaining. She is exceptionally restless and clumsy, has

Doreen

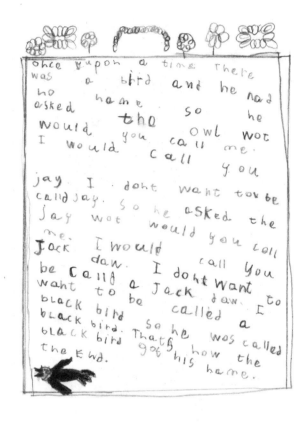

Once upon a time there was a bird and he had no name. so he asked the owl wot would you call me. I would call you jay. I dont want to be calld jay. So he asked the Jay wot would you call me. I would call you Jack I dont want to be Calld a Jack daw. I dont want to be called a black bird black bird. So he was called a black bird. Thats how the got his name. the End.

Gerald

Gerald is also eight, but you'd never think so to look at him. He is small and immature for his age and although he talks well, his reading and writing and his drawing is like that of a much younger child. His IQ is just 100, but he barely scores on a reading test.

Gerald is the youngest of three and the only boy. He seems to have been a somewhat unexpected afterthought for a mother who has always found life full of surprises (usually unpleasant ones). Gerald was obviously one of the good things and he has spent his eight years like a young lord with his mother and his much older sisters fulfilling his every whim and never crossing him.

The effect of all this is that he is babyish and unable to settle to anything much or to concentrate on anything for long. He has accepted school discipline reasonably well, so long as no one expects him to go on working when the teacher isn't looking. He blossoms in a one to one situation and ceases to thrive in a one to thirty class and usually ends up distracting other children.

Gerald made very little progress in reading and writing until quite recently. He now recognises a number of words and knows the sounds of quite a number of letters. If pressed he can build three-letter words. He appears to forget very quickly and he gives the impression that he has a poor memory. In fact his short term memory is probably normal, but he isn't interested enough to make the effort needed to remember for long. He doesn't really seem to see much point in reading and writing is a tremendous effort still.

His distractability makes him a great trial to his teacher.

difficulties in all manual skills and in concentrating on anything for long. Her teachers sometimes describe her as delightful and sometimes as infuriating.

Her slow progress in reading so far seems to be the product of poor manual skill in writing and inability to concentrate. She is now making more rapid progress with a quiet and sympathetic teacher but can't be too bothered with detail. She is a great guesser and comes up with some strange answers from time to time. She has now grasped single sounds, but has not yet learnt enough blends and digraphs to use phonics to decode and build longer words. She also has some difficulty in breaking words down.

Gerald

I do two stories every day now.

Me

Michael

Michael is a twin. His mother has recently had a mental breakdown and has great difficulty in coping with her children. She has spent a good deal of time in hospital and Michael and his brother Joseph have been passed around the family circle of relatives and friends so that they are now, at five and a half, pretty insecure children. Neither parent gives much time to the children and the twins have become dependent on each other. Joseph is very much the dominant twin. He talks for them both when he is allowed to and Michael will do very little without him. Both children are small and immature for their age but Michael is smaller and more immature than Joseph. Michael talks very little at any time. He answers questions with a word if he answers

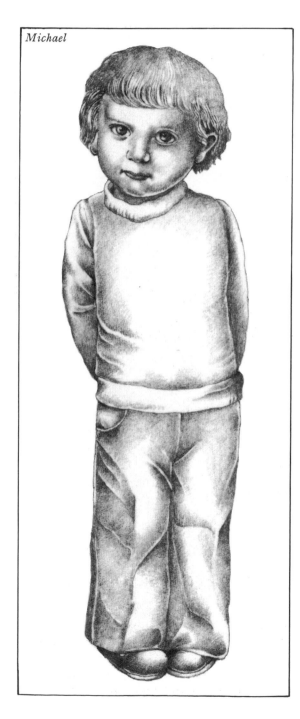

Michael

at all and rarely volunteers a comment. He looks to Joseph before he does anything much.

Everything that Michael does suggests that he is of fairly low intelligence, except that his manual skill and ability to draw are about normal and better than one might expect for his size and immaturity. He is slow to understand what is said to him and shows little progress in work on the beginnings of number. He finds classifying and ordering very difficult and has only just learnt to count rather uncertainly to five. After nine months in school, in a small class with a good teacher, he does not yet appear to recognise any written words.

He rarely plays with anyone other than Joseph and refuses to do anything at all if separated from him.

The next two children, Paula and Ranjit, are alike in one thing only. They don't speak English at home. But while Paula after eight months still has hardly enough English to express urgent needs, Ranjit at seven, is more English than the English. Their needs are therefore quite different.

Paula

Paula

Paula is five and a half and is Italian, the elder child of a farm worker, with one baby brother. Her parents speak practically no English – she was even brought to school on the first day by an Italian neighbour because her own mother did not feel she could cope with the English required to register Paula. It is probable that she hardly heard English spoken before she came to school because her home is comparatively remote and the family go out very little.

At first Paula found school a great strain. She was helped a little by an older Italian boy, but he was in another class and she was alone but surrounded by English boys and girls and their English teacher. Her tension was such that she was sick on various occasions and almost the first English phrase she mastered was 'I feel sick' which gave rise to fevered activity all round after she had been sick once or twice in various unfortunate places.

After two terms she has begun to settle into school and has begun to acquire some rather quaint English in which Italian constructions get mixed up with local idiom. She is clearly confused still by pronouns and uses *he* and *she* indiscriminately. The past tense sometimes eludes her, but she has grasped the basic way it is formed in English. Her vocabulary is increasing very quickly – more quickly than her ability to put it into sentences. She still poses communication problems from time to time.

She has begun to recognise a few written words but *Breakthrough* is the main scheme in use in the school which puts her at a disadvantage in one sense since it offers fewer models than traditional schemes. She needs a lot of help from the teacher.

Ranjit

Ranjit was born in India and came to England with his parents when he was two. His parents, unlike Paula's parents, found a house where all their neighbours were English. This meant that all the family had to learn English and Ranjit was perhaps more fortunate than many Indian boys because his mother decided to work part time outside the home and she made many English friends. His older brother and sister also made English friends and learned quickly and well. Ranjit thus grew up

Ranjit

> Dear Mrs Dean,
>
> I do a Lot of work at school and at the end of school I am very tired. And now I will tell you what I do. I sometimes do ten Pages of writing and my sums and flechewr and my writing practise. And I do P.E. And I do a picture after I have done. my writing.

hearing English on every side and came to school keen to learn.

Ranjit has an IQ of 110 and his reading age on the *Young group test* is 8·5. At seven he is a joy to teach. His parents have stressed to him the importance of getting a good education and he wants to fulfil their expectations of him. He soaks up information like a sponge and is prepared to go on working at something for far longer than most children of his age. He reads fluently and writes well. His spelling is nearly always correct and even his mistakes are understandable. He rarely causes trouble and seems to be well liked by the other children.

He says he doesn't find it difficult to speak English at school and another language at home. He is aware that languages don't correspond word for word, however, and says that his home language lacks some words which we have in English. It is perhaps significant that the example he gives of this is the word *play* for which he says he has to use the English word at home.

Paula and Ranjit represent the extremes of immigrant children. Paula makes great demands on her teacher, Ranjit very few.

Alan

Alan is now a lanky near nine-year-old who is just beginning to make some progress in reading, after a stage when his parents, his teachers and he himself had nearly despaired.

Alan comes from a good middle class home, where his parents have encouraged and helped him and in which the conversation level has been high. Alan has an IQ of 114 and he speaks intelligently though he is shy and talks slowly and he has a fairly wide vocabulary. When he started school his teacher expected him to learn easily and for a long time over-estimated his progress because his conversation was good though often hesitant and his behaviour intelligent, but eventually it became clear that he was not making progress in reading and writing.

The headmistress and the teacher with responsibility for language work spent a great deal of time trying to discover the causes of Alan's difficulties and ways of helping him. Testing of sight and hearing showed both to be normal, but his level of visual discrimination and both visual and aural memory were very low. This was useful information but did not account for the hesitancy in speech, which became more pronounced as he grew older. It was also clear that his own interests matched his intelligence and that he was at odds with himself in not being able to read as well as his peers. He needed to be able to read well to

Alan

> Once upon a time
> there lived a
> boy and he was
> very naughty. One
> day he saw another
> boy the naughty
> boy's name was
> Peter. Peter jumped
> on him and a
> fight was on. the
> other boy won
> and Peter Never
> was Nasty again

satisfy his learning needs, and his motivation
was very strong indeed. He would work
desperately at anything which looked like
meeting his problem.

His teacher described the speech hesitancy
as 'searching for the words he needs'. He also
showed some difficulty in sorting out word
and letter order and it began to emerge that
one of his major problems was sequencing.

Alan was fortunate in that his school was
able to provide daily work in a small group
for him with a very able and experienced
teacher who was expert in language development. He has gradually overcome many of his
earlier problems, but is still a long way behind
his contemporaries and his own reading needs.
His present reading age is just 8·0 years.

Each of these children poses problems for the teacher which are peculiar to him or her. Ranjit is probably the only one who can get along with very little personal help. The others all need a measure of individual attention and some will need a good deal. None of them has problems serious enough to need special education and most don't even warrant work in a special class.

These six children are not as it happens, in the same class, but every class contains their counterparts. There are few classes in first and infant schools which do not contain children like Doreen, with high intelligence but low performance, and many have children who find it difficult to concentrate. Most classes with five-year-olds have children like Michael who apparently have very little language. There are lots of children like Gerald who lack the will to work. There are those like Alan with poor discrimination and poor sequencing skills. Many teachers too cope with children of foreign nationality whose command of English may vary from nil to fluency.

These six studies serve to emphasise the need to organise so that individual needs are met. This does not mean that all work should be individual, but that the programme must take individual problems into account. It should not be a matter of processing every child through the same programme but of having a programme which is flexible enough to meet each child's needs.

How many children in your class have pressing individual needs? How far are their needs similar to those of these six children?

How does one meet the needs of children like these in a class of thirty five or so? Let us first look at what is involved in meeting their needs as individuals.

Approaches for different children

Doreen and Gerald are both very restless children and part of the problem in each case is inability to concentrate. The teacher has two tasks here. She must see that they learn in spite of their distractibility. She must also work to improve their powers of concentration.

Children like Doreen and Gerald need a greater variety of approaches to learning than other children. It is no use starting with the view that it will do them good to get down to some hard grind. It may help up to a point, but it will wear out the teacher before it is effective, and they will probably learn less and stand less chance of becoming independent learners than they will if more gentle methods are used.

With children like these, you need to seek out the things they enjoy doing and the methods that bring the best results in terms of their learning. In particular you need to discover things they will work at without you standing over them, so that they don't claim more of your time than you can give them.

Many distractible children find it easier to work where the sights and sounds of others are cut off. Booths and carrels can be improvised or made and offer a useful retreat for them – almost like blinkers (see next page).

It often helps such children to work with tapes and headsets from time to time since this cuts them off from sound and creates a

Booths and carrels can be improvised or made, and are often very helpful to children who are easily distracted.

kind of one to one situation though of course this cannot replace the actual contact with the teacher.

Both these children will probably learn more easily from games, slide/tape materials, programmed learning, *Language master* and *Audio-page* programmes and individual apparatus, than they will from books and work cards, although these must have a place (see also part 4, page 129). When you discover something that works with this kind of child you need to cash in on it all you can.

Using the interests of these children is helpful and may carry them over some hurdles, but they nearly always need to get down to learning particular skills like sounds, since they tend to not pick them up in the course of other work. They need more motivation than many children to learn in areas where they have very little natural interest. You may also need to be more systematic and do more checking with them.

Being systematic doesn't mean that you sit a child down and insist that he goes through a programme in the order you say. For children like Doreen and Gerald this would be counter-productive. It means that you need to be very well organised in your thinking and clear in your own mind about the sub-skills involved in learning to read and what the child you are helping actually needs. You also need to have your materials well organised so that you can immediately lay hands on what you need and you need several pieces of material to teach each sub-skill.

If you are organised in these ways, you will be able to see that a child who lacks concentration uses his time to good effect because you will be matching the material to his learning needs. If you have more than one way of teaching a particular thing, you will also be able to match his learning style and give him material likely to interest him, at least for a short time. This variety of material will also enable you to come back with a different way of teaching him the same thing if he doesn't get it the first time.

This kind of system is really needed with all children, but it is the slow learner and the disorganised and distractible child who suffers most if he doesn't get it.

A check on Gerald's actual knowledge shows that he has not yet learnt the hundred most used words (key words). He has some knowledge of initial consonants and short vowels, but this is not complete and he cannot yet use them to build new words. He has still some difficulty in identifying sounds within words, and he has scarcely begun to recognise blends and digraphs. It is also probable that he has a very inadequate idea of what the process of reading is about and is not entirely at home in the language we use for talking about reading. For example, he does not yet know what we mean when we speak of a *capital letter*. He has difficulty too in generalising from one word to another, so that a rule like adding *–ed* to the verb works for him in one situation but he seems unable to transfer his learning.

Gerald's teacher therefore has several different tasks in helping him to learn. She needs to help him to see that reading can be enjoyable. The easiest way to do this may be to put reading material of the appropriate level on tape. By listening to it and by getting some sense from the text he can then practice reading himself so that later he can try and read to the teacher. It will also be important to involve him in small group work where stories are being read aloud and constantly to be offering him the pleasures and values of reading.

His teacher will also need to think clearly about the language she is using in talking about reading – *word, letter, sound, symbol, blend, full stop, comma,* etc. and check that he really does understand these words.

Tape could also help him in hearing sounds in words. Stories on tape might bring out words with similarities. Picture cards in sets of three or four of objects all starting or ending with the same sound, with an odd one out, can be sorted with help at first from the tape. The *Stott games* can help a great deal here and children usually enjoy them. Programmes from *Tutorpack* (Packman Research Ltd) may be useful. He is also likely to be attracted to programmes on *Audio-page* and *Language master* machines which should help him to hear and eventually to blend sounds.

Doreen is much further advanced than Gerald. She reads quite well and enjoys it and she knows all her single sounds. She can blend well, but has yet to learn the blends and digraphs. She too would benefit from work with tape, but because of her distractibility rather than from any problem in listening. *Stott* and other games would be useful to her too as would various kinds of programmes for learning the phonics she needs. The worst of her problems are over and the task is now one of continued learning and consolidation.

While this learning is continuing with these two children, the teacher must start to tackle the problem of their inability to concentrate. One way of doing this would be to talk with each of them about the problems of concentration he or she is meeting and explain the effect of this on learning. The teacher will then need to get each child involved in working with her to overcome the problem. Each day she needs to find time to agree some targets with these children which are just within their reach, and set up a record for them in a personal notebook showing how they are doing in reaching their targets.

For example, the teacher might agree with Gerald that he would write a whole page at one go without getting up or talking to anyone. Doreen might agree to work at a piece of book work for a given time by the clock which is placed where she can watch it. If they reach the target, they can mark it in their notebooks. If this is not sufficient incentive, the reward of choosing an activity might be offered.

It is very important in using this technique to show your awareness of how the child is doing at the time when he is attempting to reach his target. If you aren't around to offer praise when he achieves it, the technique will rapidly cease to work. It is also important to get the target right – just difficult enough to be challenging, but easy enough to make success likely. If the child doesn't succeed one day, make the target a bit easier the next, so that he does succeed. The technique only works when he is successful most of the time.

How do you cope with the problems presented by children who seem easily distracted? What other methods or techniques might children like Doreen or Gerald benefit by?

Michael poses a quite different set of problems, which have something in common with Paula's. Both children need a lot of opportunities for

to him. He might also profit from working at something which involves explanation with a carefully chosen partner. Most of all he needs time to talk with the teacher.

What other approaches would you offer Alan?

These six children are all very different. There will be some areas where some of them at least will work easily and happily with others, but each of them except Ranjit needs other work which is more individual and takes account of his or her needs. The teacher's problem is to organise in such a way as to make this possible.

Organising for individual need pre-supposes opportunities to study individual need, to discover problems like poor auditory memory or poor sequencing. A great deal of teaching effort can be wasted if this kind of information is not available. Obtaining it may be none too easy in a large class, unless you make a particular point of collecting and recording the information you need.

The task of collecting information about children starts as soon as you know who will be in your class, and it is useful to start a ring file with a page per child to which you can add information as it comes your way. It may also be helpful to have your list of objectives in this file, so that you can note each child's progress towards them.

How much information you collect in advance depends on your opportunities for collecting it and your views about what it is useful to know. If you are taking children from another teacher in the school you can ask questions easily, but if you are taking in children from home or from another school your opportunities may be fewer. A good deal of information only begins to make sense when you have begun to know the child.

What information about children would you like from the teacher who had them last? Are you spending valuable time discovering what she could have told you?

It may, nevertheless, be useful to consider the information which may be available to you from colleagues and parents in the following areas:–

● Background information – date of birth, information about home background, country of origin, home language, any handicaps of sight or hearing, any serious illnesses or gaps in schooling, right or left handedness, colour vision, etc.
● Development – information about the level of physical, social, emotional and intellectual development compared with peer group. Motor skills.

● Attitudes and interests – what does he enjoy doing? What brings good responses? What does he react badly to?

● Skill and knowledge in school work – level of conversation, books read, level of reading and writing skill, etc.

What relevant information might parents be able to offer about their children's language development when they start school? Is it possible to organise so that teachers have enough time to find out what information parents can offer?

Once children start working with you, you can add to this knowledge through observation. You will also be able to observe developing social competence, study skills and independence in learning, personal organisation, degree of personal control and overall attitudes as well as the development of specific skills and concepts of the acquisition of knowledge.

A great deal of this information will be picked up in the course of day to day work with a child if you know what to look for and it is worth giving considerable thought to ways of doing this. Collections of errors and miscues in reading may provide information (see part 3, page 104). You may notice a child having difficulty in copying or in the manual skill of writing. Language difficulties will reveal themselves as you talk with children and you will learn about their attitudes and interests from their reactions to different situations.

What clues to language development should you look for when a child is first in your class?

You will also need to do some systematic checking of things like understanding of the language we use in teaching reading, phonic knowledge, visual and auditory discrimination and visual and auditory memory and so on. You need your own collection of material for doing this. For example, to check auditory discrimination you will need a collection of groups and pairs of words, so that you can ask a child questions about similarities and differences. In some cases too, you may need specific tests to help you to make judgements (see part 3, page 93). You need a record for each child which shows you at a glance the areas he has and has not conquered. Five or ten minutes each day devoted to checking where individual children are will pay real dividends in your ability to provide for their needs. This is especially true for the children who are not making progress. It is much more important to make this kind of assessment than to test for reading age, since it can give you clues about what to do next.

Where you have a child with a really difficult problem and there is no organisation in the school to find out the causes of the problem or the areas of difficulty, it may be possible to agree with a colleague for one of you to take both classes for a story or some other large group activity while the other attempts to discover the difficulties of individuals. It is both time-wasting and often ineffective and damaging to the confidence of a child with serious difficulties to work on trial and error in what you offer him. You must get down to the nature of his problems and try approaches which take account of his strengths. It may help to ask yourself the following questions. (Many of them could be incorporated in the check list described earlier on page 19):

● Is his sight and hearing apparently normal? If you have doubts about this you should ask for tests to be made.

● What is his speech like? Does he articulate clearly? Does he speak in sentences? Are they simple or complex? Does he use past and future correctly? Does he use pronouns and prepositions? Does he get words in the right order?

● Does he understand the words you use to talk about reading, e.g. word, sentence, sound, symbol, etc.?

● Can he trace over/copy from a work card? copy from the board? write unaided? Does he form letters correctly? Is he right- or left-handed?

● What sight vocabulary has he?

● How good is his visual discrimination? Can he pick out details in letters and words? Can he match shapes? 1, 2, 3, 4 letters?

● How good is his auditory discrimination? Can he hear differences in pairs of words like *view* and *few; dimmer, dinner; reef, wreath*, etc.? Does he recognise rhyming words?

● How good is his visual memory? Can he hold in his mind and recognise again a group of 2, 3,

4 or more letters when shown them briefly? Can he reproduce them?

● How good is his auditory memory? Can he repeat sequences of 1, 2, 3, 4 or more letters, numbers or words?

● Does he have sequencing problems, i.e. does he get words and letters in the wrong order?

● Can he hear sounds in words?
Can he write the symbols for given sounds:
single consonants
short vowels
long vowels with –e
two-letter blends and digraphs
three-letter blends and digraphs

● Can he build words? Can he decode?

● How does he set about reading to you? What mistakes does he make?

Neighbourhood and parents

You not only need to take into account the needs of individuals, you also need to look at the overall composition of your class which reflects the neighbourhood of your school. If you have a class which has a full range of social background and a full range of ability you probably need much more varied approaches than you do if the group is more homogeneous. In this kind of group the most able will set standards and provide models which you can use to everyone's advantage, but you will need to see that they work at the peak of their capacity. This kind of group is at its most difficult when you have children at both extremes of ability and social background and few in the middle. In a school where classes tend towards this pattern, there is a good deal to be said for pairing classes and dividing the children between the two teachers for more intensive work on particular needs at some

point each day, and leaving them mixed for all other work.

There is now a good deal of evidence which suggests that the less able a child is, the greater his need for systematic work in learning to read. If you work in an area where children have had fairly limited opportunities for talking and looking at books before they come to school, where parents make rather different demands on them from the school, you will need a very clear, straightforward organisation as a basis for your work and you will need to establish ways of doing things that free you to work with individuals. Your programme will need to include a good many incentives and opportunities to explore different kinds of talking and you will need to organise so that it is possible to talk with small groups. You will also need to work hard at introducing children to books and reading.

If, on the other hand, you have a class with a lot of articulate and demanding middle class children, your task is no easier, but you need to work differently. Many of these children will learn fairly easily because you probably talk the same language as their parents and their homes are reinforcing your work all the time. They need extending however and you will find that you need to be well organised in a rather different way to keep them going. There will also be some who do have difficulties, which is often made worse by the expectations and demands of their parents and their own feelings of inadequacy compared with their peers in the same class. These children may need more help and support than the child whose parents have not such high expectations. They may need very systematic work as well as a great deal of your time.

What is the language experience of the children in your class? Which children have been

48

encouraged to look at books and have been read to? Which children appear to have had a good deal of conversation with adults?

The parents of your children affect their learning in many ways and we know from various studies that home background is the biggest single factor affecting a child's ability to benefit from education. The Plowden Report, *Children and their primary schools*, suggested that there was a considerable resource available to the school in the parents and that very few parents were really uninterested in their children's progress, although some found it difficult to approach the school because of their own unhappy experiences of schooling.

What activity will you need to provide to complement home experience?

The amount you are able to make use of this resource must depend on the policy of your school, but it is certainly worth considering whether there is any contribution which the parents of your children could be encouraged to make in or out of school which would help the children's learning. For example, could they hear reading at school or at home? Has any of them a particular skill or interest which the children would enjoy hearing about?

The Bullock Report, *A language for life*, also laid great stress on the importance of educating parents for their role in supporting the language development of their children and experiments appear to show that one of the most effective ways of helping a child's language development is to help his parents to help him. While it can be argued that the role of the school is to teach the children, it is nevertheless worth looking to see whether anything can be done to help parents to help them.

If you have parents helping you, is there anything you can do to help them to add to the children's language in the course of activities?

In some schools, for example, parents assisting with activities such as helping children to change for swimming have been asked to try to introduce various pieces of language to the children as they help. Other schools have made suggestions to parents about out of school activities which might help language development. It would be possible to arrange for small groups of parents to watch and discuss a BBC programme like *You and Me* which makes positive suggestions about ways in which parents can help with language development. Exhibitions of children's books and discussions about them may be helpful. Much of this work is best done on a fairly small scale, often with parents, teachers and children doing things together and discussing them.

How does the neighbourhood you serve affect the work of your school? How far should the language programme be geared to meet the needs of the children and how far should it be concerned with levelling up the work of children from different backgrounds? Is there a basic standard which everyone should reach?

Could you make more use of the resource that parents offer?

Some parents complain that teachers act as if the parents have little information of value to offer them about their children. Is this view justified? Do we treat parents as partners in educating children?

You and the rest of the school staff

Teachers vary in the degree to which they see their classrooms as private kingdoms, but no

Below: knowledge is sometimes better retained when a child has to make some effort to find out. Finding out with this chart involves lifting the flap to see what sound the letter represents.

a relationship with a child so that he wants to read in order to please his teacher;

● to give practice.

How do you rate the importance of these different objectives?

Each of these purposes needs careful consideration if the time spent in hearing individual reading is to be well used. What can be learned from hearing a child read is dealt with in detail later in this book, but the last two objectives listed above need further consideration here.

Children learn best when their relationship with the teacher is good. Individual relationships are established best in one to one situations and when you hear a child read you are concentrating on him and his particular needs and this helps to build the relationship. Most children, for their part, want to please their teacher and are anxious to show themselves in a good light. They are rarely fooled by reassurances when they know they are not doing well. It is therefore important for the teacher-child relationship for at least some of each child's experience of working individually with the teacher to be experience of success and it is an important part of the teacher's task to break down what is to be learnt for each child so that he can succeed in something at least. When you hear a child read you need to ask yourself what positive reinforcement you have been able to give.

If the answer is none, then you need to think how what you are asking the child to do can be broken down further, so that he achieves success. This is always possible. You have only to reflect that many children in ESN (M) and even ESN (S) schools learn to read to realise that the slowest child in your

56

Below: a reference wheel for sounds. This is made from two circles of card fastened in the centre with a brass paper clip. By turning the top circle to the appropriate point the child can reveal a picture which gives a clue to the sound the symbol represents

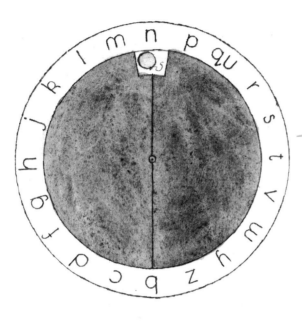

opportunit
as talking.
sufficiently
to learn.

It can b
work to st
you may
experienc
to underst
example,
mathema
which you
vocabular
include in
narrow an
describing
square, tr
words lik
and many
language
in asking
to learn a
centimetr
also be so
angle, sy
related t
if childre
meaning

This k
informat
likely to
of the w
need to
your wo

What ca
other are

Teachi

In looki
learning

class has enormous potential if only you can find the particular keys to learning for him.

Children at a certain stage in learning to read also need practice. At the early stages they need to practise recognising words in a variety of sentences. A little later, when phonic skills are developing, they need to practise recognising words from the phonic clues. This practice needs to be at a slightly lower level than the stage a child is working at, and a listening ear for practice can be provided by anyone who can read. It doesn't really require a teacher, because it is a different activity from those described later in this book. Parents can help here, either in school or at home. Older children in the same school or from a secondary school can help. So can students. Children can also do a good bit of practising with a tape recorder, listening and following the text of a book. They can also help each other to practise. Lots of practice is needed and if the teacher controls the situation it is not difficult to make good use of volunteer

helpers. You need to see that the reading material for practice is at the right level – a bit easier than the material the child is studying. You also need to spell out for the helpers what the task is. Children need encouragement. When they stumble it is probably best if the helper simply supplies the word so that they get the feel of a continuous text and develop an interest in what it says.

Although hearing children read is an important part of the teacher's role, it will not, by itself, ensure that they learn to read, particularly if other children waste time while you hear reading. Many teachers feel a permanent sense of guilt about their inability to hear children read as often as they wish which can result in hearing reading for short spells in ways which don't really forward learning all that much. It may be better to aim for some reading or writing activity with you each day, individually or in a small group, and to do a more thorough job when you hear reading.

Teaching reading will also involve work with small or large groups introducing parts of the reading scheme, using flash cards, playing word building games, work with apparatus or work sheets geared to individual need. It may involve class or group teaching and practice of word building and word recognition, and of sentence building. You will need to teach children the use of the various conventions used in writing such as question marks, exclamation marks, full stops and commas. They will need to recognise and use capital letters. These too are best learnt in small groups when children seem to be ready for the information.

These aspects of reading can be learnt in a variety of ways, but your organisation should provide opportunities for individual, class and group teaching and practice, with and without him to set his own goals and become properly involved in his progress towards them.

What makes a child want to learn?

What can we do to involve children in planning their own progress? Do we do enough of this?

What opportunities are available at school for children to read and write for real purposes and real audiences?

A child will see some point in learning to read and write when there is immediate purpose in it. He will make tremendous efforts to discover what something says if what it says will enable him to do something he wants to do or find something he needs. He will work hard to read letters addressed specifically to him and may be ready to try hard to reply to them. You need constantly to be looking for *real* occasions for reading and writng.

It is also motivating to be faced with a problem to solve within one's capacity, and this can be exploited. A child who is asked to see how many words can be made with a given group of letters, or to collect words of a certain kind and try to discover a rule about them, is more likely to work at the task and remember what he has learnt than one who has been given the information and told to learn it. One way of judging materials and activities is to ask how far they enable a child to reason on and tackle problems for himself. Do they help him to become independent of the teacher? Do they help him to make generalisations about reading which can be applied in new situations?

Children will also be motivated by competition, and games in which they are matched so that all the players have a reasonable chance of winning are very useful.

Gadgets like the *Language master* where something moves or lights up are attractive and likely to provide incentive, and sometimes the impersonality of a tape recorder can provide an opportunity for practice which doesn't involve showing the teacher the mistakes one is making. Programmed learning also offers motivation for some children because it presents information in very small steps in which almost every child can achieve success. It also presents the correct answer immediately after the child has written his answer, thus reinforcing the learning.

The most important element in motivation is undoubtedly the teacher. Young children learn through their feelings and are very sensitive to the atmosphere created in school. The teacher is very powerful in their world and her good opinion of them is of great importance. The most successful teachers of reading somehow manage to give every child the confidence to take the next step.

What is best learnt by direct teaching and what by personal exploration and discussion?

Grouping children

If you have a very small class it is possible to plan a programme for each child and work with him. Some work will also be done in a larger group or else the children will miss out on the stimulus and range of language models that this affords, and even in a very small class you will want children to work together for some activities so that they develop skills in communicating with each other.

In most classes it is very difficult to plan as individually as the teacher might wish and some grouping will be needed for some work. There are several ways of doing this.

60

● You can group together those who are at about the same stage in learning a particular skill. This can be an ad hoc grouping or semi-permanent.

● You can group children so that you get a productive mixture of personalities.

● You can group – or let children group themselves with their friends.

There is a place for all these kinds of groups.

How and why do you group children in your class?

There has been a good deal of muddled thinking about grouping children and teachers often react against any kind of ability grouping because they have seen the damage that too early and too sweeping assessments can do. Nevertheless we have to acknowledge that there are some pieces of learning which are linear, where you need to learn stage by stage. There are other areas of learning where you can start in any number of places. Each child needs to go through the necessary stages of a linear pattern of learning and ideally work of this kind should be individual for much of the time. Many of the sub-skills of reading are of this nature. You can't get far with learning phonic blends until you have learnt to hear and recognise individual sounds within words. You won't be able to understand and make inferences from a text if you can't read the words.

Which parts of the language programme need a linear treatment and which can be more open?

On the other hand a group of children at a wide variety of stages of reading may discuss a story or plan a piece of drama and may contribute as well or better than children who are more advanced, and everyone may benefit from the language of others.

It is therefore important to differentiate between the learning that must be linear and the more open kinds of learning and to group differently if you want a group to whom you can teach a skill from the group where you want a more creative response. There is, in any case, some advantage to the children in having a range of language models available to them. If they do all their work in an ability group, they lose the opportunity of learning from other children.

To what range of language models have children access? What determines how they use these?

Is there a place for ability grouping in language work? What are its advantages? What are its dangers?

Linear work in the end must be individual, because a child's understanding of each stage depends upon his understanding of the previous stage and it can be argued on this basis that ability grouping will never be needed. There will simply be individuals at different stages and groups will always be mixed ability. In any class, however, there will be occasions when it is sensible to teach something to a group at the same stage in the linear parts of the programme and it may be helpful to have groups which come together fairly regularly for this kind of purpose. These groups may also be useful for giving out the work to be done. You may be saying *Children in the blue group are to do the next four cards while I work with those in the red group.* Each child will actually do the four cards next in his programme, but the grouping provides an easy way of giving out work. The important thing is not to fix permanent labels on children which easier to spend time *monitoring* what they are doing and their understanding of it. Coding will also enable you to say *Take any material with a blue triangle on it* or *Read any book with a red star on it* or whatever your code may be knowing that this will be at a reasonable level for a given child.

What do your children do when they finish a piece of work?

Some of the language work you ask children to do will be related to work in other curriculum areas, perhaps arising from visits or television programmes, or work you have started in a class group. You may also have various kinds of exhibitions in the classroom or in the school generally, which may start children talking and thinking and which may become the basis of work in reading and writing. Very often it is possible to put out written suggestions for work as part of an exhibition. You can therefore suggest work from one of these sources in fairly general terms. *Write about our visit to the fire station* or *Find out more about the animals we saw on television yesterday* or *Choose a work card from one of our exhibitions.*

These kinds of suggestions can be made in writing for groups or individuals without too much trouble and without limiting children too much. Other work may start from work with you and the written programme the following day may say *Go on with the work on sounds we started yesterday.* On other occasions work will arise from individual conversation with you or a child will come to school with some idea he wants to work on. There should be room for this too.

The programme can be written on the board if you wish, but there are advantages in giving it in other ways. If, for example, you use

sheets of paper, put up in strategic positions for different groups you can take them down and file them as a record of the work you planned and you can add comments where necessary about what happened or about work which arose in the course of the day.

The daily work you plan for each child should contain elements of fairly systematic work designed to help him master particular aspects of reading. Phonic skills come into this category. It should also contain elements of freer and more creative work and for children past the very beginning stages some work from books and some writing. You also need to plan some work for each child when he is working directly with you, individually or in a small group, and some work where you are working with the whole class.

What proportion of a child's time in school should be spent in language activity?

As I have already said, time is the one commodity in school which remains constant. Every so often you need to ask yourself questions about the way in which you are using your time and the way each child is using his or her time.

Are you spending too much time answering questions like 'Where's the scissors?' where a better organised classroom environment would avoid the need for such questions?

Are you spending too much time with particular children and not enough with others? If so, it may help to plan to pay particular attention to a particular group of children each week, and to consider carefully whether the demands which some children are making of you can be met in any other way.

Are you saying the same thing over and over

again to different children? If so should you perhaps do more with groups.

How much time are you spending doing work with children that could only be done by a professional teacher?

How much time are you spending on helping children to think, reason, plan, create; how much on stimulating and inspiring and encouraging?

You also need to look critically at the way your children are using time. It can be useful to pause and look at what is happening at a given point and ask yourself some questions.

How many children are working profitably?

How many are wasting time?

What does the work of an individual child add up to in the course of a day or a week?

Is it enough for a child of his intelligence and stage of development?

Most teachers of young children probably devote about a quarter of the total time on language work, although it will in another sense be part of all the work children are doing.

What proportion of his time should be spent in specifically language activity and what proportion on other work?

Space

Space is also partly finite. You can usually only re-arrange the space you've got, although it's sometimes possible to find extra space by changing the use of corridors, cloakrooms, and cupboards. Nevertheless it is often possible to get better use out of the space you have by organising work in a different way.

The use of space is tied up with the use of time and the grouping of children. If you want everyone working at the same thing at the same time this limits what you can do with the space available. If, for example, you really feel that it is essential for every child to sit at a table at one and the same time, you are committed to a table and chair place for everyone. If you can manage without this you may be able to dispense with some of the furniture and make more space for other things.

You need to arrange the space and furniture you have to provide spaces for:–

large group discussion with you, including the whole class;

small group discussion and work with and without you;

individual and paired work with books, work cards and work sheets, other apparatus, audio visual equipment

Large group discussion is probably best carried out with the children seated round you on a piece of carpet and many schools now have this facility. If you haven't a carpet and see little prospect of getting one, you might consider raising funds to buy carpet squares which can eventually be laid to make a carpet. Large cushions, particularly those of the foam rubber variety make good seating in such an area, and it can also be used for individual work.

Work with small groups requires corners and bays which can easily be made with cupboards, trellis, corrugated card and various other things. Even without bays, groups can work round tables or on the floor.

Individual and paired work may simply require table space, but it may need power points if audio visual equipment is to be used. Carrels and booths have advantages here, and

Carrels can be specially made. Trellis and
corrugated card can be used to make bays or they
can be used for display.

It is generally best to centre each activity on one
part of the classroom or area adjoining, and to plan
the organisation of your materials very carefully
within that area.

can use it to gather the whole class or a group for discussion and teaching. Individuals, pairs and small groups will also use it for reading and some writing activities but it will be necessary for these to spread over into other parts of the room where there are tables and chairs.

You could make the book area with one wall of open shelving on which you set out a good deal of the reading equipment and apparatus. Or you may like to make one wall into a place where you go to work with audio visual equipment, perhaps making carrels by putting sheets of board between tables. Children using the equipment are best facing the wall and this helps to use space economically.

Sometimes an adjacent storeroom or space near the classroom can provide some room for work with audio visual equipment. You need to see what possibilities are available.

If you work so that some children are in the shared work space for much of the day, you will have space in the classroom for individual and small group work. Obviously it is important that you plan with your colleague who shares this space, so that she uses the work space when you are working with your whole class and want them together and conversely. There will also be times when children from both classes use it together.

An important element in your planning is to display. Most classrooms now have a fair amount of pin board, but there is never enough. You can add to what is available by using corrugated card in various ways, however.

It is really better not to display too much at once, but to change displays fairly frequently and make real use of them. A number of ideas about adapting the physical environment are given in books in the series *Room to learn* by J. Dean published by Evans.

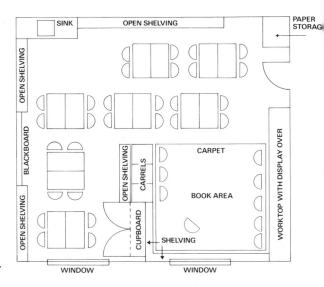

What are the advantages and disadvantages of having particular areas for particular activities?

What are the problems of not having a table and chair place for each child?

Materials and equipment

If you had a teacher for every pupil and infinite time, you could use almost any material to teach a child to read. After all he learns to talk in whatever context he finds himself and the raw material of his early language development is the world around him.

Very few children have a teacher to themselves for much of the time and most teachers are therefore dependent on their materials, some of which will be published, some of which will be home made. It is, nevertheless, important to remember that materials are there to support the teacher in the programme she is planning to meet the needs of a particular group of children. They should not dictate the programme. It is also important to work from first hand experience as well as from materials so that children see real purpose in what they are doing.

The next step in your planning is therefore to look at the teaching equipment and material that is available to you. If you are working in the room you had last year and have the same things available, you are at an advantage, but even then it might be worth asking whether there is anything new in the school which you might use.

Do you know the range of resource material available in your school?

If you are making a survey of what is available for the first time, in your own classroom or elsewhere, it's worth collecting everything you have for the teaching of reading and trying to classify it in a similar way to that suggested for the whole school on page 25 classifying materials broadly under the headings of pre-reading, word recognition and phonics. You then need to go on from there to fill the gaps. Try to fill a gap every time you make a new piece of material. It is terribly easy to make what you need for a particular child on a particular occasion and never to find time to build your stock up so that it really covers all you need and is readily available.

What kind of coding do you use in your classroom?

An important part of the provision in most schools is the reading scheme. Many reading schemes today provide a wide range of material in addition to the books. They also offer a fair degree of structure and so are a very valuable basic resource for the teacher. It is possible to do without a reading scheme if you have few children and a great deal of time to make material for them, but it is probably not the best use of your time when you can buy in the product of somebody else's thinking.

A reading scheme and its ancillary material is never enough by itself. The grading it offers will not meet the needs of every child. Some will be able to work through it quickly. Others will need a good deal of additional material at each stage to establish their learning. Some will also find the reading scheme material uninteresting and will need other stimuli. It will also be important to have many other books available, so that children are attracted to books and do not get a false view of what reading is about. It is, perhaps, significant that many children and some teachers talk about a 'reading' book or a 'reader' as if it were different in kind from other books. There is a need for structured material for learning to read but reading must be concerned with content. Technique is only a means to that end.

The reading scheme or schemes are thus an important part of the total language programme not the whole of it. Each teacher needs to think out how she will provide for each child's development and learning in relation to the overall language programme.

What is the place of a reading scheme in the language programme?

Some children need many approaches to one piece of learning before it is really established. Some will learn well with one approach and less well with another. It is therefore useful to aim at having several varied kinds of material for teaching each skill. For example, you might put a programme on initial consonants on tape, and you might have several games designed to reinforce this knowledge. You might also have individual apparatus and work sheets and programmes

Books are a very important part of the material available to you, and we have already seen that you need many more books than those in the reading scheme. Some of these will contain pictures with very little writing. Some may be home made by you or by the children. Others will have text of varying degrees of difficulty and as I have already said there is a need to have a grading and coding system for these too, preferably on a school basis. This will be a different system from that for materials, but could also use colour as a simple means of differentiating. This should not mean that children look only at books at their own level. Many may wish to browse through easier or more difficult books, but for much of their work, they could be encouraged to choose books which they can manage.

Equipment for language work today should also include cassette recorders and playback machines, perhaps with a junction box and head sets so that a group of children can work together on a programme. A tape recorder makes it possible for a teacher to duplicate work she would otherwise have to do herself, particularly work which depends on listening. Children with auditory problems often find it difficult to get enough practice in listening for things they find it difficult to hear and a tape recorder is invaluable to them, since it allows them to hear the same thing as many times as they wish. Playback machines are all that is needed for this purpose and these are much cheaper than recorders.

Tape can also be used with slides which can be projected or seen in a hand viewer. There are a number of extremely cheap viewers on the market now some of which use natural lighting and don't require batteries.

The *Audio-page, Language master and Card reading machines* are all highly desirable additions to classroom equipment which enable the teacher to go a bit further than is possible with ordinary tape.

Radio and television are also important language resources. Radio programmes of stories and poems can be taped and heard many times by individual children and small groups. Most of the material of this kind of broadcast for schools is accompanied by pamphlets giving the text, so this offers a valuable source of high quality and well-presented material which can be used many times.

The same is true of school television programmes where a school has a video tape recorder. Even without this, however, broadcasting offers an extension of what the teacher can offer and a variety of language models which is very valuable.

Displays

Another very important part of the classroom environment is provision for display. Display is a teaching tool in many senses. It may be the stimulus or starting point for work. You might, for example, build a display of brown things, or Victoriana, or wooden things, or you might set out the processes by which men work with a lump of raw clay and turn it into cups or plates. These displays need some written explanation and some invitation to children to add to them or do work from them, perhaps demanding careful observation or exploration outside school or in books. You will also want to use them for discussion.

Some displays will be the end product of a piece of work and you will build up the display as you go along, with children writing captions and explanations and contributing their work. This kind of display can sometimes be drawn together at the end to make a package of material for other children to work on. The children themselves may contribute some dis-

Display is a valuable teaching tool. Classroom
display boards can be augmented with corrugated
card. Three-dimensional display is also needed.
There should be provision at different heights.

*Language materials need to have suitable
containers so that they stay tidy and in order.*

Wall pockets, boxes and plastic bags on hangers are
useful for flat materials and work cards.

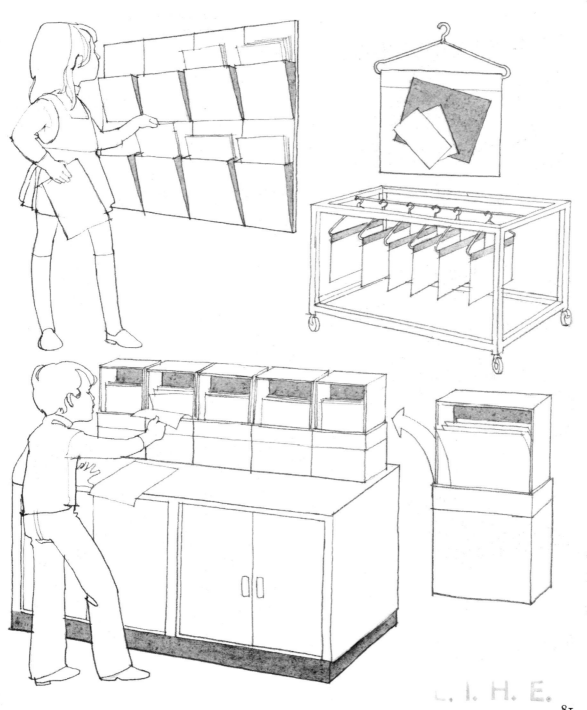

you can make a slot to hold books by fixing a one-inch square batten to a wall and then fixing a two-inch-wide strip of hardboard or clear plastic along the front;

this kind of shelving can be fixed on both sides of hinged wall panels;

you can buy wire book racks;

you can buy or make a book trough for large books (old locker desks with the legs cut down and dividers can be used for this and so can old cupboards laid flat).

● Special storage (see page 84). Some things, like felt pens and scissors, really need their own special storage. Writing tools are usually best stored in racks. These can be made from old boxes or jars can be used. It is a good idea to have writing tools at a number of points in the room.

Scissors are best in a special rack or a wall board made for the purpose.

Rubbers and sellotape are less likely to disappear if you attach them to a large piece of wood and hang them from a board.

Paper is often difficult to store satisfactorily. Large paper needs a paper storage unit, but can be hung from a line. Smaller paper is probably best kept in trays or circular containers.

One further important element in your organisation is labelling. Label everything that needs it in writing which is clear to the children. Make lists of what should be on each shelf and stick the list to the shelf. This then makes it possible for each child to have a small area in the classroom to check when you are clearing up. It also provides a way of finding where things are.

You can take this a bit further by including lists of the pieces in each box of material.

Where it is possible to draw the outlines of pieces inside a lid or on a separate piece of card, as well as labelling them, you have a checking device which every child can use and which provides the youngest with practice in shape recognition.

What kind of storage arrangements do you have in your classroom? How can you improve things?

Record keeping and evaluation

However you work and whatever your organisation, you need to keep records and evaluate your work from time to time.

The major part of your record keeping will be your records of the progress of individual children and many suggestions for this have already been given. You also need to record in some way, how each child is actually using his time, the books and equipment he is using and his day to day progress with them. Many teachers provide a card for each child to use in working through books of the reading scheme on which they note the pages a child reads to the teacher. Books completed can then be listed in the teacher's file.

Materials used can easily be recorded if each piece of apparatus is coded. The codings can be entered, possibly by the child, on a chart which the teacher checks frequently and compares with her own record. The easiest way to do this is to put up a sheet of file paper each week for small groups of children. They can then draw or stick shapes or write other coding against their names as they use material and the sheets can be collected by the teacher at the end of the week.

With children towards the top of this age range it can be valuable to get each one to keep a record of his own work each day which you discuss with him from time to time. You

Books can be stored and displayed in many ways.

*Paper can be stored in a circular container – a
large tin useful for pieces of paper for writing – or
it can be stored flat.*

*Writing tools and scissors and other small things
need appropriate containers.*

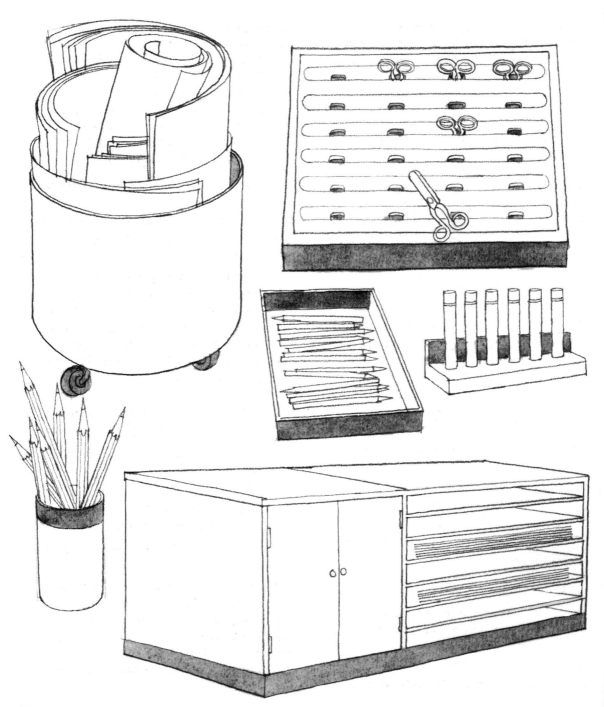

need to give time to this, however, and teach children how to do it. Another way of recording by children which brings in planning skills is to give each a planning and record sheet on which he enters the work he intends doing and ticks it off when it is finished. You then initial and comment when you check the work. These sheets can then go into a file and will provide you with an on-going record.

Another way of involving children in their own progress is for each to keep a file of work he considers to be good. This involves discussion about what goes into it and the file itself becomes a very good record of the child's work.

How does a teacher learn what to expect from each child? Is there a danger that we underestimate children?

Every teacher also needs to evaluate her own work. You will, of course, be doing this by assessing each child's progress, but you also need to be asking yourself questions about how effectively you are using the variable factors in the teaching situation. The following questions may be worth asking.

How far does your classroom environment stimulate language activity?

(a) Are there situations in which children actually need to read to do something?

(b) Do the displays invite contributions?

(c) What learning opportunities are there in the environment which don't entirely depend on you, the teacher?

How much are you doing which helps children to extend their use of language, not only in vocabulary, but also in language structure and ways of using language?

(a) What models are available to them?

(b) Are you doing enough to involve them in

talking for a variety of purposes, e.g. reporting and reflecting on experience; anticipating, predicting and planning? comparing courses of action; explaining how things happen.

(c) Do your children get enough opportunities to practice the social uses of language e.g. entertaining visitors, answering the telephone, thanking, enquiring, apologising, etc.

Are you doing enough to encourage children to read?

(a) How many of your children read for pleasure?

(b) How many ask to take books home or belong to the public library?

(c) How much time and effort do you give to choosing and preparing stories and poetry to read to your children?

(d) How much do you encourage children to use books as part of their work? Have they the necessary skills to do this? What do they actually do if they want to find out something from a book?

(e) What sorts of attitudes to books and reading are you encouraging? What effect is this having?

Is the programme of language work you are providing adequate for the needs of your children?

(a) Does it provide adequately for speech and listening as well as reading and writing?

(b) Do you know what your objectives are for each child?

Are you using the resources you have available as fully as possible?

(a) Are you and are the children using time to the best advantage?

(b) Are you making the best use of the equipment and materials available? Is any of it not much used?

Reading Record

Name Michael Hong

Date of Birth 19·1·68

Reading Age 7.2 (Schonell)

Books   Sounds

Rodney 3·12·75
Tree House 12·12·75
Puppet Penny Made 22·1·76
Cherry Television 30·1·76
Bread & Butter House 27·2·70
Indyo 18·3·76.

a	3 letter words	
b	4 letter words	
c	sh	✓
d	ch	
e	nk	
f	ck	✓
g	ing	✓
h	ong	
i	ung	
j	ang	
k	th	✓
l	oo	✓
m	ee	✓
n	ea	
o	ai	✓
p	ay	
q	oa	
r	ar	
s	or	
t	er	
	ir	
u	ur	
v	ow	
w	ou	✓
x	y	
y	ies	
z	aw	
	au	
	all	
	silent e	✓
	" b	
	" w	
	" g	
	" gh	
	" k	

Note errors, refusals, reversals and give separate attention,
do not continue with books in Reading Scheme if errors are
repeated and reading hesitant. Find out why.

Michael is becoming more hesitant with his reading
and naughtier in class. I am worried that
he is being pressured at home and feels
upset that he is behind his sister.

(c) *Can the children find what they need without asking you?*

(d) *How much material have you which is self correcting or can be used without your help?*

(e) *Is the space used as fully as possible? Could you get better use of space by organising differently?*

(f) *Are you using resources inefficiently by the way you plan the programme?*

How good is your provision for the slowest and least able children and for the most able children?

(a) *How much of the day do they spend profitably?*

(b) *How adequate are the materials you provide for them?*

(c) *What are your objectives for each one? Could they go further than they do now?*

How adequate is your record keeping?

(a) *Have you a sufficiently detailed knowledge of each child's progress?*

(b) *What will the next teacher be able to learn from your records?*

(c) *Are you using a format which takes as little time as possible and gives as much information as possible?*

Case study

We asked Mary I'Anson who teaches at Vineyard Infants School in London to tell us how she organises her children and her classroom and to describe the events on one particular day

Background
I have a class of thirty-five six and seven-year-olds, mainly from middle class, professional backgrounds. Most of the children, therefore, come to school with obvious language-literacy advantages. I run an integrated day, i.e., a variety of activities run concurrently and the children have a certain amount of choice about their work load and the timing of it. Teaching is done, as far as possible, on an individual basis. There are certain fixed points during the day around which we work: two main class discussion-teaching times, which never vary; break-times and group activities such as watching television, listening to radio, drama, assembly, cooking, sewing, swimming, writing practice, etc. which vary from day to day.

We have active, interested parents whom we encourage to help in school. I have five parents who come into school on a regular, weekly basis to take cooking, embroidery and knitting, swimming, writing practice (a teacher/parent takes this) and another who hears fluent readers.

We are housed at present in an old Victorian grammar school, totally unsuited to infants. We moved here because our own school was found to be built with 'high alumina' cement.

Classroom organisation
I believe that one of the most important things in running a successful integrated day is to make sure that your classroom environment is well organised. At the beginning of the year, whether I have moved classrooms or not, I find it advisable to 'put my class together'. I find the most helpful way to do this is to list all

the possible activities I might organise, to take stock of the space available to me and to start to build my activity areas.

This was my list of activity areas:

writing and drawing;
book corner (central meeting point);
maths;
sewing;
creative (clay, paint, junk, collage etc.);
woodwork;
brick building;
music;
house corner.

Obviously I try to separate noisy areas from quiet ones by using corridor space, which the children are taught to view as a classroom extension not as an escape unit! I also take into account the age range of my children – seven-year-olds are likely to sit down for longer periods than five-year-olds – so the size of the work areas will differ from year to year to meet different children's needs. Having 'built' my classroom I find it important to put clear notices by each area about the number of children able to work there. If your clay table is for two, four children working there can cause chaos! By the time they are seven, children are used to these constraints but at an earlier stage I find that I need to remind children rather more often if I want the day to run smoothly.

The next stage in my planning is thinking about the equipment I need to make sure that each area has its own supply of pencils, scissors, paper, crayons, etc., easily available to the children so that movement between different areas is minimised. Other standard equipment and work cards, etc., are also placed in the relevant areas. I also find it very useful to have a drawer unit with a place for each child to keep storybooks, maths books, diaries, current reading books and cards in. This advance planning takes time and energy but is really worth it in the long run.

Obviously in running an integrated day approach I need to 'know' my children – ro have a sense of direction for each child. I keep a simple diary of work done daily by each child under general headings such as maths, writing,

reading and creative work.

I also have a page for each child where I jot down relevant information about his learning abilities, his sociability, his needs and interests, his need for direction or his ability to work independently.

Our book corners have a variety of reading schemes and other children's literature. The schemes have been banded by the staff as a group into colour coding. So, for example, all pre-reading material carries a pink band, books with very limited vocabulary carry a blue band, the next stage a green band and so on. This gives the children a choice of books, something they have been used to at home, and also helps me to offer quick reliable advice to a child who wants guidance. We have many story books which are used by teachers and children and these are changed frequently. We have a reference library in the centre of our corridor which is used continuously by the children. The books are colour banded by subjects, e.g. red for transport, white for animals and birds, gold for poetry, etc. The children are encougaged to find books here for all aspects of their work. Perhaps before making a model of a ship a child will search out a book that will help him with its shape and his writing about his model. The younger children are helped in finding books by large pictures over each book rack on a particular subject.

We also have a lending library. Books are changed once a week and it is stressed that these books are for family enjoyment and a child can choose any book, not necessarily one within his reading capabilities. We review our reading schemes yearly. New books for all the libraries are bought yearly too.

My Day
8.30 a.m. My day begins half an hour before school starts and it is then that I check that all the equipment we shall need is available. I also take note of children who need to finish tasks and perhaps children who need to start tasks in one particular area or particular skill. I also check which group or groups will be leaving the classroom on that day.

9.00 a.m. The children arrive and congregate in the book corner chatting about last evening's activities, talking to me, generally familiarising themselves with their environment again. This five or ten minutes is very necessary to young children. I take the register (two children are absent today).

9.10 a.m. First fixed discussion – discuss yesterday's work and remind children of projects on the go at the moment. Then the planning for the day is started – each child tells me what he is starting with, some are told by me what they need to start with.

Today five children have writing to finish, three are writing stories, one a poem, one writing about a model. Seven children have maths to finish. Three of them are working on the conclusion of a survey, one is weighing and measuring his model, one is doing some maths work – weight, height, vital statistics, etc. – on her doll. The other two are doing a subtraction sum work-card.

Six children are going for extra language help with our 'floating' teacher. This group of children go twice a week. This week they are listening to a story on tape and following the text in a book. They will also do some work on sounds, and then some individual work according to their needs.

Three children are working on a large picture of the Battle of Bunker Hill. The other children are ready to start new tasks and two choose to write and draw about babies crying – one of our classroom topics is 'Young Babies', an interest that arose from discussion about my own pregnancy. One boy is writing a poem about penguins – another class project on 'Sea Birds' which was sparked off by a television programme. Two other boys are working with clay, they go to the reference library to find books on penguins. Two children are making cushions and following instructions from a craft book. Two children are reading to themselves, they will discuss their stories with me and read me a page. They are extremely fluent and it is not necessary for me to spend so much time hearing them read as I would with less able children. One child is reading to me. One boy is writing a book

criticism. He is a child who will sit and read all day, and I find I need to use this interest to motivate work on other skills. I suggest that he choose his favourite book of this week and allow us to share his pleasure by writing us a criticism. We have a class book of work like this which is read avidly.

9.35 a.m. All thirty-three children are working by now. This process has taken about half an hour. The children will refer back to me as they finish their activities. Sometimes this reference is short, sometimes lengthy depending on the child and his needs.

10.15 a.m. School Assembly and today we listen to poems about birds – some found in books, some written by the children. They are already familar with words like *glide, swoop, hover* from the BBC school radio series *Movement and Drama*.

10.30 a.m. Milk and a twenty-minute break.

10.50 a.m. After break we have P.E. which lasts until 11.20 a.m. The children then return to their unfinished work or start a new task, always coming to me so that I know at all times who is doing what. Of course, there are one or two children who tend to get distracted from their tasks. During the day I try to keep a special eye on them and spend a little time encouraging them when their interest flags.

12.00 noon Lunch. I ask five children to read with me. Two read their own stories, three read books from reading schemes and choose a further book, under my guidance.

1.15 p.m. Second fixed discussion – At 1.15 p.m. we meet in the book corner and together choose work to display and discuss. Today Caroline reads us her story. I ask her about her use of speech marks. We have a short class teaching session on speech marks. The clay penguins are proudly shown to the class and the two creators explain to us the differences between Emperor and Fairy penguins. The books they have used are left in the book corner for others to look at. The finished survey is read out. The whole class is prompted to give further suggestions for the conclusion and other ways of setting it out. A painting is shown, and Annabel reads the beginning of her story. I ask the class what they think might happen next in her story. Lots of ideas flow. Annabel lacks imagination in story writing and these ideas will give her much needed stimulus in a constructive way. The word list we have been making with words we have read or used beginning or ending with 'sh' is read out and a few more are added.

This coming together is a central point in the day. Today it has taken thirty-five minutes. With younger children I would gather them together more often for shorter periods.

1.50 p.m. Our work pattern then continues in the same way as the morning. The children are expected to do some writing, reading, maths and something creative each day. This usually works well but when a child doesn't manage to fit in a particular task or work on a particular skill, he starts with that the following day.

At the end of the day it will have been my aim to hear all the children read something. A whole book, a personal story, a label, a conclusion or an instruction. Sixteen of my children need more of my time daily on this specific skill than the others. All the children will have read at least one book in a week, most of them many more. The time spent on language is continuous – in most of the activities there is an element of language work present.

2.30 p.m. Break.

2.45 p.m. We return to the book corner for the radio programme, *Stories and Rhymes*. The children go home at 3.15 p.m. and after they have gone I fill out my diary, check work to be finished tomorrow, note that there is a group for swimming and cooking tomorrow too. I mount finished work and display models with labels for the children to read.

How does this compare with a day in your classroom?

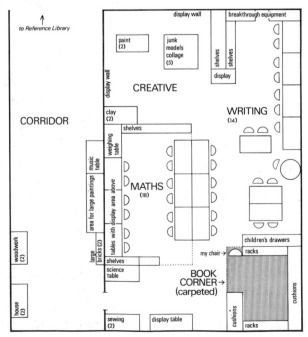

90

Part 3 Assessment

by Dr Elizabeth Goodacre, Principal lecturer at Middlesex Polytechnic and consultant to the Centre for the Teaching of Reading, University of Reading

How do you assess young children's reading abilities, check on their progress and determine where their difficulties lie in reading?

Most teachers would probably think first of the more *informal* assessment techniques based on their own classroom observations, such as their hearing of children's reading or their completion of check lists of reading activities rather than more *formal* means such as the standardised reading attainment test. Both types of reading assessment have advantages and disadvantages, and the skilled teacher is the one who can decide when each form of assessment is most appropriate and use the resulting information to further her understanding of pupils' individual learning strengths and weaknesses.

For thinking about your pupils' reading progress, you probably need to ask yourself two questions:

What will I want to know?
Will this particular technique be the best way of finding out the information I want?

What questions do you ask yourself when thinking of assessing children?

Formal methods – standardised reading tests

Standardised reading tests are usually referred to as being *norm referenced*, since they are measures enabling you to compare an individual's performance with that of the 'norm' or average score of children of the pupil's own age. When using such measures, you really need to know your reasons for undertaking this type of assessment. Do you want to know how the children you are teaching are progressing in comparison with other children of the same age? Do you want to know how the standards in your particular school in a given part of the country compare with national standards? Or do you want to know more about the strengths and weaknesses of a particular pupil, so you can devise more appropriate and effective teaching for that particular child? Do you want to know more about the range of reading abilities in your class, so that you can group them better, either on the basis of children of similar abilities working together at their own rate, or in order to provide particular learning experiences or teaching for children with obvious deficiencies?

The answer to such questions will determine whether a *survey* or an *analytical* reading test is your best choice. Generally survey type tests are group tests, designed to give information as to how the individual or the class compares with other children of the same age. Analytical tests on the other hand, can be group or individual tests but are primarily designed to supply you with useful information about a pupil's strengths and weaknesses. Usually group tests take far less time to give, but analytical tests provide more information and give you the chance to ask a child immediately after their performance on the test about their answers or to note down letter recognition or phonic difficulties. Such information enables you to tackle particular problems and plan appropriate action, either with individual children or by grouping children according to the type of difficulty they are experiencing.

The NFER *Reading tests* (Tests A, AD and BD) are survey type tests in which the pupil has to choose from a group of alternatives the correct item to complete the sentences that are read silently. Whereas tests such as the *Neale analysis of reading ability*, the *Carver word recognition test* or the *Thackray reading readiness profiles*, although providing information on individual readers' performance levels, also provide you with information which has considerable diagnostic value.

Once you are clear as to why you want to use a standardised reading test, the next step is to find a suitable one. This is not such an easy task in this country as we do not have the reference type publication of the *Mental measurement year books* (Buros) as produced in the United States – periodically updated this publication gives the details of cost, content and publisher and critically reviews tests as they come on the market. This absence of test information is mainly because there simply is not the same amount of test publication being carried out in this country, especially in regard to appropriate forms of assessment for young children. Probably the most comprehensive account of reading tests now produced in this country is the book by Peter Pumfrey (1976), *Reading: Tests and assessment techniques* – a UKRA Teaching Reading Monograph published by Hodder and Stoughton. It provides a wide range of information on both British and American tests and considerable guidance for the teacher seeking particular types of tests. The table on page 93 lists reading tests suitable for use with children aged five to nine, drawing only upon reading tests published in this country.

Which standard reading tests do you use and why?

For a number of years there has been a certain suspicion among British teachers, especially infant teachers, of reading tests. It is sometimes suggested that 'the time could be spent more profitably teaching, than wasting time in testing'. Certainly teachers of young children should evaluate published reading tests for themselves and assess their value. For instance you must consider whether the content of the test reflects your understanding of the reading process. A test of word recognition can tell you how a particular child goes about pronouncing a word when there are no contextual clues, but it cannot reveal anything about the way in which the child reads for meaning or enjoys an exciting story. It is useless to expect more from a reading test than that which it sets out to do!

If you are considering using a standardised reading attainment test you should consider such things as the cost, not just in monetary terms but also in terms of your time; whether the instructions and the procedure involved in the test will be suitable for your pupils or is likely to cause anxiety or worry; whether you can understand the administration and marking procedures of the test, whether the test is intended for your children's age group; whether the publishers have produced a manual for the test which says something about the test's *reliability* and *validity*.

The reliability of a reading test is the consistency or accuracy with which a test measures what it is designed to measure. The test should be so constructed that you have confidence that the score obtained today will be similar to that obtained if the test is repeated shortly afterwards. The analogy of a piece of elastic is sometimes used. This would be a very poor measuring instrument, since it can be stretched and will provide different measurements on different occasions. Similarly, if the instructions for a reading test are not clearly stated, teachers may interpret them differently and this test would not be a reliable measure of pupils' reading abilities.

To ask if a test is valid is in effect to ask how good a particular test is in measuring what it claims to measure. For instance, *content validity* of a test is the way in which it matches up to the content of what is being taught. A test is a valid measure of pupils' attainment if the

Content of reading tests	
This chart classifies tests in terms of their overall approach to reading and the language level involved in the reading tasks asked of the pupils. This classification may help the teacher to choose an appropriate test in line with teaching objectives.	
Code emphasis (often reading aloud) mostly individual tests	**Reading for meaning** (usually silent reading) mostly group tests
Word level Oral reading; graded lists; recognition; spoken words; phonic knowledge and skills *Burt-Vernon graded reading test* *Schonell graded word reading test* *Carver's word recognition test* *Southgate test 1* *Domain phonic test kit* *Jackson's phonic skills* *Swansea test of phonic skills*	
Sentence level Oral reading of graded sentences *Holborn reading scale* *Standard test of reading skill (Daniels & Diack)* *Salford sentence reading test*	Matching sentences with pictures; sentence completion *NFER tests, A, AD, and BD* *Gates-McGinitie comprehension* *Young group reading test* *Spooncer group reading assessment* *Southgate tests 2* *Wide span reading test* *SPAR tests*
Passage level Oral reading passages of graded difficulty; speed and accuracy *Neale analysis of reading ability*	Multiple choice; matching; completion; cloze; rate of comprehension *Edinburgh reading test stage 2* *GAP reading comprehension test*

* Based on a descriptive grid by Denis Vincent in NFER Educational tests bulletin No 5, Autumn 1974

READING TESTS FOR YOUNG CHILDREN (5–9 years)

Burt-Vernon graded word reading test Hodder and Stoughton Educational 'to, is, he, up,' etc.,
Age range 4–15 (superceded by the Burt word reading test).

Carver word recognition test Hodder and Stoughton Educational. Up to 8·6. Types of error made provide diagnostic information.

Domain phonic test kit Oliver and Boyd. Age range 5–9. Battery of five diagnostic tests, four phonic knowledge and one similar to Wepman test of auditory discrimination

Edinburgh reading tests Hodder and Stoughton Educational Age range 7–12·6 (when range complete)

in four stages. Stage 2 (8–10) and stage 3 (10–12) now available.

Jackson's phonic skills (PS tests) Glasgow: Gibson. Age range 5–9. Series of eleven tests to be used selectively, suggestions for remedial work contained in the teacher's manual *Get reading right*.

GAP reading comprehension test Heinemann. Age range 5·5–11. Test based on 'cloze' procedure, testee reads silently, writes in missing word.

Gates-McGinitie reading tests NFER. Age range 6·6–8. American test now in an Anglicised version, assessing vocabulary and comprehension.

Holborn reading scale Harrap. Age range 5·5–11. Norms only for word recognition (not recently revised), none for comprehension part.

Neale analysis of reading ability Macmillan. Age range 6–12. Accuracy, comprehension and rate, plus three optional supplementary tests. (No norms for supplementary tests).

Reading test AD NFER (previously *Sentence reading test*) revised 1970. Age range 7·6–11. Sentence completion, comprehension.

Reading test A NFER (previously *Primary reading test 2*) First year Junior. Sentence completion, comprehension.

Reading test BD NFER (previously *Reading test 2*) Age range 8·6–11·4 same type.

Salford sentence reading tests Bookbinder. Age range 6–10. Similar to Holborn but has advantage of parallel forms.

Schonell's graded word reading test (RI) Oliver and Boyd. 'free, little, milk, egg, book,' etc. Age 5–15.

Southgate group reading tests Hodder and Stoughton Educational. Test 1: word selection, age range 5·9–8. Test 2: sentence completion, age range 7–9·7.

SPAR (spelling and reading) tests Hodder and Stoughton Educational. Age range 7–15·11. Picture word matching and sentence completion.

Spooncer group reading assessment Hodder and Stoughton Educational. Age range 7·9–11·7. Three sub tests, word recognition and sentence reading.

Standard tests of reading skill (Daniels and Diack) Chatto and Windus. Age range 5–9. One of battery of tests in *The standard reading tests*. Child reads a question aloud e.g. 'is it not?' No marks for correct answer, scored as to how correctly question is read. Questions graded in phonic difficulty. Scores converted into reading ages or standards, with follow-up diagnostic tests suggested. No evidence of reliability, validity given.

Swansea test of phonic skills (Experimental version) Blackwell. Age range 6·6–7·7. Using nonsense words, tests, short and long vowels, final letter blends, digraphs, vowel combinations.

Wide-span reading test Nelson. Age range 7–15. Sentence completion, testee's choice of item can be used diagnostically.

Young group reading test Hodder and Stoughton Educational. Age range 6–13. Word recognition and sentence completion.

---

test items cover the area of knowledge which is to be assessed. The problem with reading tests is that often they are not measuring the process or the skill in the way in which it has been learned in the classroom. When that happens, such tests cannot be considered to be valid measures of that particular teacher's pupils' reading attainment.

You therefore need to look very carefully at the content of a reading attainment test to see if what it is asking pupils to do agrees with your understanding of what the reading process constitutes and presumably what you have been encouraging pupils to learn and use in the classroom situation. To use a word recognition test such as that of Schonell or

Burt to assess 'reading' progress may give a very limited and unreliable view of the pupils' reading attainment. If you believe strongly in the importance of contextual clues, the relationship between language and reading, that children should make use of their knowledge of spoken language, then this particular type of test would not be a valid means of assessing 'reading' progress for your purposes. If such a test was used, to obtain a realistic assessment of pupils' progress, it should be augmented by other measures such as a book 'criterion' assessment (what book level the pupil was at) or scores on a test such as the *GAP reading comprehension test*, which is based on the 'cloze' procedure and makes use of linguistic knowledge.

Do the tests you use reflect the approaches to reading you employ? Are they measuring the processes and skills you are teaching the children?

It is vitally important that when you are completing pupils' records, especially those which will be passed on in the educational system, you should name the reading test used when recording a pupil's reading age or score. For really understanding such records you need to know something about the reading task or type of skill the test claims to measure. Some tests are more sensitive instruments than others in regard to what the test asks of a pupil in order to score a particular reading age. A test evaluation study by Ruth Nichols (1974) found that reading tests used in the primary school age range varied considerably in their sensitivity – some asked pupils to answer only several questions to obtain a particular reading age whereas on other tests the child had to answer a number of questions or items to score at the same reading age level.

Studies of the progress of remedial children over short periods of time are often reported in terms of gains of several months in reading age, often using the Schonell *GWR test*. An increase in reading age of six months over a period of three months would suggest that a particular child has made significant progress, but such progress looks less spectacular if translated into terms of the change in test score. On this particular test, such a gain means that the child has read five words more than when previously tested three months earlier. Probably there would be likely to be a degree of test familiarity operating anyhow, if the test in the same form was given again within such a short period of time. When you are considering using a particular test for periodical checks on reading progress, it is advisable to find out whether the test has alternative forms, or test familiarity can be a factor affecting the reliability of the reading assessment.

How often do you use the same test with the same children?

Limitations of formal methods of assessment

Some of the limitations of standardised tests have already been mentioned but the main ones can be summarised as follows:

● The very fact that a test has been standardised in terms of instructions and scored in relation to a nationally representative sample, may make it inappropriate for use with particular groups of children; e.g. slow learning or ESN children, pupils with hearing defects or the partially sighted, or immigrant children with language difficulties.

● Limitations involved in producing commercially tests which are cheap, easily given and marked may produce a test which samples a very limited form of reading behaviour, and timed tests can penalise the child who works accurately but takes his own time about it.

● Group administration can present problems in the classroom where children are encouraged to help each other and such children may not take kindly to the more formal organisation often demanded by the standardised test situation; e.g. separate seating, working competitively with time restrictions, due attention being paid to practice items, being prepared to concentrate and attend to oral questions, etc.

● Easily marked tests often mean the child has to answer some form of multiple-choice questioning, and some slow or even non-reading pupils may therefore score above their real performance level by reason of chance marking of correct items.

Informal methods – or testing by doing

Informal methods are sometimes referred to as *criterion-referenced* measures as they tend to relate test or assessment performance to the mastery of a particular task or skill. They are not concerned with comparison with the pupil's peers but rather whether this particular child can or cannot complete a set task or understand a concept related to the reading process. You can use them as direct methods of assessing the effectiveness of your teaching and thus determine which children need further practice or detailed help with a particular teaching or learning element of the reading programme. Once criterion behaviours have been identified (aspects of behaviour identified as being involved in 'reading'), they can be sampled either with paper-and-pencil tests or

various informal techniques devised by you, such as the following:

● *Teacher observations:* The alert and skilful teacher notes all sorts of different information about her pupils; she may systematically observe their overall reading performance, find out about their interests and attitudes to books and reading; notice how they attend to problems and the limits of their attention in learning situations, detect physical weaknesses or eye/hand preferences. Observing in this way can provide the teacher with real insight into the problems a child may encounter when he tries to read unfamiliar words, choose a book for himself, or write legibly. For instance, the teacher who notes the left-handed child in her class who obscures the letters in words as he writes has additional information on which to draw when she sees that many of his spelling errors involve incorrect sequencing of the letters' strings. She can suggest a posture to him, which allows him to see what he is writing as he is writing it.

● *Anecdotal records and children's work:* The teacher can also remember to put to one side, perhaps in a folder with the child's name, any examples of the pupil's work which illustrate their progress or their mastery of a particular concept, or she can note down the gist of incidents which reveal particular difficulties or evidence of stages of development. Such entries and collected material must be dated. With slowly progressing pupils, it is often useful to show them their work which they have done at an earlier stage, and in this way they can see for themselves the actual progress they have made over a particular period of time.

● *Non-standardised or teacher-made tests:* Teachers quite often make use of particular exercises from the workbooks accompanying

Below: an example of an inventory of tasks, which provides a record of individual pupils' laterality.

Laterality

Background

It is useful to test the hand and eye dominance of children because, although the evidence is sometimes confusing, there has seemed to be a slight association between confused laterality and reading failure. However, there are many cross laterals (people with the right hand and left eye dominant, or vice versa), who have learned to read.

Left-handed children are at a disadvantage in our right-handed classrooms and often need help. Eye and ear preference may affect visual and auditory recall and can show up in spelling mistakes, as well as being involved in scanning of words and lines of print in reading.

Instructions

Ask the child to carry out the following tasks. Do the items in the order below and shade in the appropriate squares:

	I	R	
1 Put a toy telephone in front of him and ask him to answer it. Which ear does he use?			(ear)
2 Look through a rolled-up paper telescope or kaleidoscope. Which eye does he use?			(eye)
3 Ask him to pretend to comb his hair. Which hand does he use?			(hand)
4 Ask him to kick a ball – tester throws the ball towards the child. Which foot?			(foot)
5 Ask him to cut with scissors. Which hand does he use?			(hand)
6 Ask him to hop on one leg. Which leg?			(leg)
7 Ask him to look through a keyhole. Which eye?			(eye)
8 Pick up a pencil and write his name. Which hand does he use?			(hand)
9 Put a watch on the table and ask him to bend down and listen to it. Which ear does he use?			(ear)

Summary

Overall preference (underline or circle appropriate category)

Strong R / R with L tendencies / L with R tendencies / Strong L

Specific preferences (use R (right), L (left), or M (mixed))

Hand=   Eye=   Foot=

Dominance (Hand/Eye/Ear)

All R / All L / M – specify the last . . . .

Cross lateral Hand (used for writing) / Eye

Not cross lateral   R/L   L/R   Mixed   R/M   L/M

---

reading schemes or the completion of different reading games and aids, as informal testing procedures. Books containing crossword puzzles, word and picture-matching games, sentence completion activities and many other specific teaching points can be obtained and mounted on cards covered with a protective film or kept in plastic wallets. For instance, all the work to do with initial consonant blends or the 'magic e' rule can be collected from various sources and thus provides the child (with an uncertain grasp of the particular rule or concept) with the additional practice necessary. Accurate record keeping on the part of the teacher will ensure that the child who understands and can effectively use a particular rule will not have to become bored by unnecessary practice.

● *Check lists:* These forms of assessment seem to have grown in popularity over the past decade and are really mainly a way of making teachers' observations more systematic. In this somewhat general category, can be included such things as interest and personality inventories; questionnaires of work habits and interests; and lists of specific skills which can be used to check a pupil's mastery of specific areas of knowledge. Joan Dean and Ruth Nichols' book *Framework for Reading* (Evans, 1974) is a most useful source of such check lists. (*Framework for Reading – Check Lists* by Ruth Nichols provides printed spirit duplicating masters of the check lists). One difficulty which can arise with the use of such check lists is that the teacher or user may not interpret items in the same way as the designers of the check list intended. For instance, in checking on children's language development, teachers of different social background, might very differently interpret the item 'still uses baby talk', while other teachers might be at a loss

as to how to interpret in practical terms the item 'does he *appreciate* rhyme in such words as bell, shell, sell?', an item checking on auditory discrimination in a reading readiness check list.

● *Hearing children read:* Probably this is the most common form of informal assessment carried on in classrooms, certainly in the early stages of acquiring the skill. The teacher 'hears' the pupil read aloud as a means of checking both their progress through a book or reader, and their efficiency as a reader – or in other words – *how they are doing.* However, teachers on the whole rarely are explicit about their objectives or their criteria of progress in the hearing situation. Reasons suggested have been to diagnose difficulties, to help with unknown words by discussing them in context, to draw attention to the code aspect of words (sounds of letters, etc.), to estimate the extent of the reader's understanding of what they have read, to reinforce the personal relationship between the teacher and the child, and to check on the accuracy of the reading. Work I carried out some years ago, suggested that many teachers emphasised the last aspect of the situation, placing considerable emphasis on oral reading which had some of the characteristics of speech – use of pitch and expression, few mistakes and no re-reading or backtracking in the text. Fluency of reading was seen as evidence of understanding. Since then work by such people as Clay, Goodman and Smith have shown that a child's mistakes or 'miscues' are not something to be eradicated but rather evidence of the child's learning strategies and their stage in acquiring the skill. As hearing is such a popular form of assessment in the early stages, I shall return to this topic again before the end of the section (see page 104).

Informal reading inventory

More popular in the United States than in this country, is the *Informal reading inventory* or IRI. This is usually a number of graded extracts of reading material, produced either commercially or by the teacher using duplicated passages selected from the various levels of the reading scheme used in the school. The teacher chooses a passage and then records the number of mistakes made as the pupil reads aloud.

Four levels of reading ability can be identified through use of the inventory:

● *independent level* – the level at which the pupil makes few if any mistakes, but usually not more than one word in twenty, can understand the vocabulary, and answer correctly questions on what they have read.

● *instructional level* – makes errors at the rate of not less than one word in ten, but not really sufficient mistakes to interfere with the meaning. May not know some of the words used if asked about them after reading the passage, but has probably some impression of their meaning from contextual clues. (This may lead to misconceptions of course, which is reflected in the ability to answer questions about the passage.) Needs some help from the teacher, although it is not always easy to know when this can best be offered. Interruptions to draw the child's attention to a teaching point, may interfere with the pupil's reading for meaning.

● *frustration level* – more than one word in ten being misread, and interfering with under-standing of the meaning of the text. Probably a number of words are unfamiliar (often nouns or verbs) or the conceptual ideas may be too abstract to be easily understood. Possibly only able to answer about half the comprehension questions asked although it is now realised that the *types* of question asked are very important; i.e. literal or inferential, the latter raising queries regarding the part played by 'intelligence' in the pupil's ability to answer.

● *listening capacity level* – the highest level at which a pupil can understand at least three-quarters of material which is read aloud to him.

Children are usually asked to read aloud, beginning at the easiest level (independent) and continuing until the material is too difficult as according to the criteria outlined for the frustration level. The pupil is then considered to be at the level of reading difficulty indicated by the instructional stage, and is encouraged to choose books from this particular grade or reading level.

It has been found that class teachers frequently underestimate the difficulty level of the material pupils are being asked to read. The use of an *Informal reading inventory* can make you immediately aware of the discrepancies between your estimation of the difficulty level of the test and the actual level experienced by the young reader. Too many children, often with the teacher's help and insistent prodding and prompting, flounder along at the frustration stage getting little reward from the situation and simply learning that reading is hard work!

Sometimes the prose passages in published *Informal reading inventories* are accompanied by word recognition lists composed of the vocabulary of different reading books in schemes, and it is suggested that the child's performance on these indicate the level of difficulty or the particular passage he should be asked to commence reading in the IRI. In this country, I found that many teachers use the word lists at the back of the readers in the controlled-vocabulary type of reading scheme as a means of assessing a pupil's readiness for the next book in a scheme. I found that teachers varied considerably in what they accepted as successful performance by their pupils. Some insisted that every word had to be pronounced correctly and failure led to the child being asked to re-read the whole of the reader so as to gain this level of competence. Others only asked for a proportion of the word lists to be read accurately – a token performance before graduating to the next book in the scheme. It seemed to me, that some teachers were somewhat inflexible in their attitude to success in this form of assessment, and that having to get all the words right could have a disastrous effect on children's interest in reading.

It is worth noting therefore the results of a study by Kenneth Goodman (1965) on the way in which children were able to recognise a higher proportion of words in context than when appearing in a word list. The table shows the average number of words missing in a list and read correctly in a story context.

Grade	Aver. missed in list	Aver. missed in context	Ratio
1: 6–7 yrs	9·5	3·4	2·8:1
2: 7–8 yrs	20·0	5·1	3·9:1
3: 8–9 yrs	19·8	3·4	5·5:1

It can be seen that as the children progressed and grew older, they could identify more words in context which they had been unable to read in isolation. Even among the younger children, two out of three words not read in the word list, could be read when met in continuous prose.

In some schools, teachers are required to use the word list type of reading test (Schonell, Burt, etc.) to obtain reading ages for record forms. Some teachers seem to mechanically score the words pronounced by the child, add up the words said correctly, and work out the child's reading age. It would be far more use to make a note of the child's mistakes, as this will provide insight into the kinds of difficulties he is experiencing. One can make a test form, with spaces under each of the words, in Schonell or Burt, so incorrect responses can be recorded exactly as the child says the word. This information is particularly valuable for identifying letter reversals or inversions, or phonic work which may be needed. Here are two examples of children's attempts recorded in this way. Only the first thirty words of the Schonell test are shown in each case (page 101).

Limitations of informal methods of assessment

Testing by doing or criterion-referenced forms of assessment do have certain limitations, of which you need to be aware.

● Some objectives just do not lend themselves to this form of assessment. For instance, is it always possible to measure the enjoyment derived from reading a story or the level of experience conjured up by the images in a particular poem? There is some danger that such hard-to-measure qualities may be undervalued just because they cannot be measured and used as evidence of progress. As a top infant class teacher, I can remember the wistful complaint of a colleague who took the reception class, and who used to bemoan the fact that she never saw the product of her labour – 'it's in your class that they really read – you can see them reading BOOKS!' For her the concrete evidence of children getting through books, devouring pages and pages, was very important, far more than the story telling and reading, the book making, and writing activities, which made possible

ANTHONY   CA = 7·3 years   RA (Schonell) = 5·1

tree	little	milk	egg	book	school
—	*like*	—	✓	*ball*	*bus*
sit	frog	playing	bun	flower	road
said	*for*	*phone*	—	—	—
clock	train	light	picture	think	summer
—	*in*				
people	something	dream	downstairs	biscuit	shepherd
thirsty	crowd	sandwich	beginning	postage	island

Although Anthony has done very little on this test, his answers suggest that he may just be beginning to recognise words and really only looks at the beginning of the word (l – like/ little; b – ball/book; s – said/sit; f – for/frog; p – phone/playing). The last one of these, 'phone' is rather extraordinary. His own teacher would know whether there was perhaps a flash card with this on it, in the Wendy house? He can find small words in bigger words – 'in' in 'train' – a technique suggested in schemes but not always a successful aid for unlocking words. The words he has supplied might well be those he has seen in the early stages of his reading scheme. The teacher would probably recognise this fact if they were. Children in the early stages often give 'sight' vocabulary words beginning with the initial letter for words on these sort of lists.

MARTIN   CA = 7·2 years   RA (Schonell) = 6·0

tree	little	milk	egg	book	school
three	✓	✓	✓	✓	✓
sit	frog	playing	bun	flower	road
skit	*for*	✓	✓	✓	*runned*
clock	train	light	picture	think	summer
cock	—	—	—	*take*	✓
people	something	dream	downstairs	biscuit	shepherd
but/please/put	✓	*down*	—	—	—
thirsty	crowd	sandwich	beginning	postage	island
—	*call*	*sand wash*	*began*	*put*	—

Martin is just a bit more advanced in his word recognition skills – he too looks at the beginning letters, but also sometimes at the end letter. (s – sit/skit; runned/road; cock/clock; take/think; down/dream – similarity of 'm' and 'n' shape). An important stage is reached when children realise it is important to look at the second letter in words to determine the beginning 'sound' of the word. Martin is not doing this (three/tree; skit/sit; cock/clock; take/think; call/crowd).

their progress and love of reading in my class. The number of pages read to teacher, the books completed in a scheme are measurable, recordable facts but are not necessarily evidence of increasing pleasure in reading or the making of language one's very own which in turn will shape thought and learning.

● Objectives involving the retention and transfer of what is learned may become secondary to the one-time demonstration of mastery of specific contributory skills. A pupil can happily read through a list of examples of the 'magic e' such as *pile, stile, while, smile,* and *vile* and then fail to read the word *file* in the sentence *Mother took out her nail file.* Is this a word recognition problem or is *nail file* an unfamiliar concept to this particular child? What if he does read *file* successfully, but doesn't know the term?

● How should you determine proficiency in the skill being tested? Do you, as with the word lists in the back of readers, require total mastery for proficiency to be attained? Probably perfect or near-perfect performance should be the goal, *if* the behaviour being learned is an essential part of the total skill, or if the learner has experienced difficulties in this particular area previously, which have had an effect on his progress.

● Difficulties can arise in trying to determine the goals of assessment and the specific means of assessing success in a particular area. For instance, auditory discrimination is known to be important in learning to read, in hearing the sounds in words, but more recent work on measures such as the Wepman test of auditory discrimination suggests that low scores may be related just as much to children's lack of understanding of what is required of them in the test situation than an inability to hear whether the tester is saying similar or different-sounding pairs of words.

Because informal approaches tend to use such a wide variety of procedures to assess reading performance over a number of different occasions, it is perhaps not surprising that they tend to be more reliable and more valid measures of young children's reading attainment than standardised reading tests. After all, the more behaviour that is sampled, the more likely the assessment is to be accurate.

However, one of the major shortcomings of classroom assessment stems from incomplete knowledge of the reading process and the factors which are likely to interrelate to influence it. Tests are often developed, interpreted and given to children as if reading ability was a skill which had no relation to the individual's experiential and environmental background, the classroom organisation, the teacher's educational attitudes, the teaching materials used, etc. If any of the following should be altered, undoubtedly reading performance would change: the subject content of the reading material (e.g. introduce more books of special interest to boys); the purposes of reading (e.g. suggest football results should be looked up in the national paper); the reading conditions (e.g. introduce cushions, suitable small chairs, a carpet to the reading corner as well as books); the difficulty of the reading material (e.g. introduce a system of grading or show children how to use the 'five finger test of readability').

Most published tests are designed to reveal *what* a pupil can do and not *how* he does it. Only recently have reading researchers begun to focus on the reading process. Until a theoretical construct of reading is developed and substantiated, the value of testing devices to the teacher of young children, may well be somewhat limited. However, once reading is more accurately defined the avenues for test

Below: part of the 'GAP reading comprehension test' showing the deletions which have to be completed in this type of text based on the 'cloze' procedure.

development will broaden; it will be possible to develop criterion tests geared to assess how well an individual reads on the basis of what reading is rather than on the basis of how others perform this activity.

In the meantime, the cloze procedure (a method of determining a pupil's reading comprehension of a particular passage by eliminating every fifth word and asking the pupil to supply the missing word) seems to be a testing method more closely resembling actual reading behaviour. However, cloze techniques do not seem to allow the test designer to examine the inferential, reading, thinking abilities of the test-taker as effectively as well designed multiple-choice techniques. The *GAP reading comprehension test*, based on this idea, presents a series of seven short passages with certain words omitted. The pupil has to fill in the gaps with those words which he thinks most closely fit in with the meaning, and scoring is on the basis of the answers given

---

Long ago in the land of Sweden there was .... little girl who sang. She sang with the .... as they chirped in the hedges. She .... with the wind as it sighed in .... trees. She sang in time with .... own footsteps as she skipped along the country lanes.

Once there was a king who had three sons. .... was called Hussein, one was called Ali and .... third son was called Ahmed. The .... also had a niece who lived .... them in the palace. She was a very beautiful .... and all three of the king's .... fell in love with her.

When an atomic bomb explodes, the energy released is .... tremendous that in a fraction of a ...., a few pounds of uranium can give enough heat to destroy a city. If a method .... be devised for obtaining this wonderful store .... energy in a steady stream instead .... one devastating explosion, atomic power could become .... of the greatest forces for peace instead .... the most dreaded weapon for war.

by 'good' readers. Wrong spelling is not counted and the test is timed at fifteen minutes. It is intended for the age range 8·0 to 12·0 years, and is really most useful for rating of the more fluent, silent reader although pupils' written answers can supply a certain amount of diagnostic information to the teacher experienced in giving this test.

You can use the cloze procedure as an informal technique of assessment to further the reading ability of the 'high' flyers. You can discuss with the children the reasons for the words they choose for the gaps in the text, and thus come to some understanding about their reasoning and understanding of what they have read.

For the teacher of young children on their way to becoming competent, silent readers, hearing probably remains the most effective informal technique.

Miscue analysis

Reading miscue analysis was begun in 1963 by Kenneth Goodman in the United States for the express purpose of providing knowledge of the reading process and how it is used and acquired. It is his belief that this knowledge, in turn, can form the basis for more effective teaching reading techniques.

Miscue analysis is part of a pervasive re-ordering and restructuring of our understanding of reading which is happening now. It is a form of assessment contributing to the development of a comprehensive theory and model of reading; in the classroom it can be used to reveal the strengths and weaknesses of pupils and the extent to which they are effective and efficient readers. It is based on a psycholinguistic interpretation of children's reading behaviour; that is, children's observed reading aloud is seen as an interaction between language and thought, as a means of making meaning out of the 'graphic display' – those black squiggles on the whiteness of paper. Goodman believes the reader has several sources of information on which to draw when reading – the *graphic* (the written or printed symbols); the *phonological* (the corresponding speech sounds); the *syntactic* and the *semantic* (grammar and word structure) aspects of language. For the reader is seen as a user of language; as trying to get sense out of what he is reading. Teaching is seen then as being concerned with helping the reader to become efficient and effective in this task.

Goodman, and his colleagues therefore believe that nothing the reader does when reading, is accidental. Mistakes or as he prefers to call them *miscues*, when the reader reads something different from what appears in the text, are the reader's attempt to process the print to get at meaning. Goodman suggested that if we can understand how the reader's miscues relate to what is expected to be read, we can begin to understand how the child is using the reading process.

Here is a sentence* from a story used in Goodman's research, and the miscues the pupil made when reading it. (You will find a code that I use for reading miscues on p. 107.)

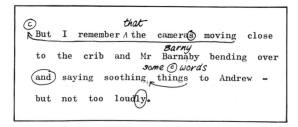

*K. Goodman 'Miscues: windows on the reading process' in *Miscues Analysis* edited by Goodman, ERIC Clearinghouse on Reading and Communication Skills, NCTE, USA.

In this sentence the reader leaves out a word and some parts of words, substitutes other words, goes back at times to correct himself, and ends up with a meaningful sentence. Goodman suggests that we should be concerned with more than his superficial behaviour. We must infer from it the process he used and his competence with that process. He put in the word *that* but corrected when he realised the pattern he had made was not acceptable grammatically. He left out *and* but did not correct this because it was not necessary – it made sense. In miscue analysis, you start with observed behaviour, but you do not stop there. You can, through analysis of the miscues, see the process at work. In this form of informal assessment, you have a window on the reading process.

What does the reader do, when he begins to experience difficulty? Usually he asks himself what would make sense, what would fit the grammatical structure (the rules of language usage), and generally then, only what would match the graphic cues – the look of the word and still fit into the meaning and structure of the sentence as a whole. This keeps the value of the graphic information in proper perspective and does not cause the reader to use any more information than is absolutely necessary.

Readers who are inefficient are often too much concerned with word-for-word accuracy which may show up as:

● Supplying a word which matches closely on a visual basis but not as regards meaning.

● Frequent correction of miscues which do not really affect the meaning.

● Several attempts at getting the pronunciation of a word right, even when it makes little difference to the understanding of the story or passage; e.g. struggling with unfamiliar character names, place names, foreign words, etc.

To assess the proficiency of a reader Goodman has suggested that it might be better to use a procedure such as the following:

1 Count the reader's miscues.

2 Subtract all those which are shifts to the reader's own dialect (reading *we was going* for *we were going*) because these are not really mistakes but rather probably the way the reader 'talks to himself' or how he thinks;

3 Count all miscues resulting in acceptable meaning.

4 Count all miscues which result in unacceptable meaning but which the reader successfully corrects.

5 Add the miscues in steps 3 and 4. The result is the total number of miscues semantically acceptable or corrected.

This last score, expressed as a percentage of all miscues, is what Goodman has come to call the *comprehending score* of the reader. He sees it as a measure of the reader's ability to keep his sights firmly on the meaning. It is a measure of the quality of the reader's miscues. What is important is not how many mistakes the reader makes but what is their effect on the meaning.

Although many teachers in this country find the idea of using pupils' reading mistakes constructively an attractive idea, there is a certain feeling that Goodman's approach may be too radical and will lead to sloppy, careless and inaccurate reading, that such an approach will interfere with the child's developing grasp of the code aspect of reading (the correspondence between letter strings and their sounds) and mastery of word attack skills.

Most teachers of young children though are concerned about the assessment of their pupils' reading progress – they are involved in judging their ability to read. But when you judge the progress of very young children learning to speak, you do this quite simply. If they can make themselves understood, they are learning to talk; if they can reply when spoken to, they are learning to listen. In other words, you judge their success on the basis of the progress they make in using language for particular purposes. Reading also needs to be judged in this way. To what extent are children in your classes learning from an increasing range of written language – reading and understanding nursery rhymes, stories, myths, legends, poetry, information books, sports results and commentaries, instructions for making things, recipes, letters, biographies, diaries, historical accounts, plays, etc.?

As Goodman has suggested:

'We let ourselves confuse published reading tests with the competence in reading they are trying to assess. The subskill tests, skill check lists, and word lists do not test ability to understand written language. They test, in large part, ability to perform with the abstract bits and pieces of language.'

Do you think that miscue analysis could lead to a sloppy or careless approach to reading?

Miscue analysis and hearing children read

Miscue analyses follow a relatively uniform procedure. A story, usually a complete one, is used which is sufficiently difficult for the pupil to make somewhere between twenty-five and fifty miscues – sufficient for any pattern of miscues to emerge. The teacher has a copy of the material to be read. The pupil is encouraged to use any strategies he knows to read unknown words, to guess or to skip a word, but the teacher does not help other than by general words of encouragement. After the story has been read, the pupil is asked to tell it in his own words. After the uninterrupted re-telling, the pupil is asked open-ended questions about any aspects of the story that have been omitted. A comprehension rating is made on an analysis of the re-telling and the miscues are coded according to a particular analytic procedure developed by Yetta Goodman. The whole procedure, reading and re-telling is taped.

This is a somewhat complicated procedure which is perhaps more suitable for in-depth work with teachers or for research purposes. But some of the basic principles can be used in the more familiar classroom hearing situation. The following ways of recording and analysing children's miscues have been used by teachers:

● The teacher can use duplicated copies of particular pages from graded reading books, recording the child's miscues on the copy and filing it as a record of progress.

● A sheet of acetate can be placed over the page in the teacher's copy of the book being read, and miscues recorded on this while the child reads from his book. The acetate can be wiped clean and reused after any particular observations are noted in the teacher's record book.

● A cassette tape recorder can be used, recording the pupil's errors during the playback. As the teacher is not involved in recording errors during hearing, she has more chance to observe other aspects of the situation; e.g. pupil's attitude, signs of fatigue, etc.

Even if this more detailed type of hearing cannot be regularly carried out, teachers have suggested that this more systematic approach and the subsequent insights into the reading process, continue to have beneficial effects on their hearing of young children. They find themselves asking questions such as 'Why did he read that? Is the meaning still acceptable even though he has made a mistake? It doesn't make sense, is he going to correct himself? If he substitutes a word, is his word the same part of speech? How close is his word to the sound and shape of the word he should have read? Why did he read *that*?'

Code for recording miscues

On page 108 is a record a teacher made after hearing one child, Martin, read in this way. It does not contain all her notes but she finally concluded that he was very dependent upon 'cues' in the illustrations in his reading books.

In this section I have tried to show you, as a teacher of young children, a variety of forms of assessment available to you. By knowing something of their value and their limitations you can more effectively choose which to use in the light of their particular needs and purposes.

Which formal and informal means of testing described above might prove useful to you?

Code for recording miscues		
Sentence to be read	**She was washing up in the kitchen**	
Error type	*Coding*	*Example*
Substitution	Underline and write in the word substituted	She *were* was washing up in the kitchen
Non-response	Dotted line under the word if reader waits to be prompted or asks	She was washing up in the <u>kitchen</u>
Insertion	Add additional word/s or part-word added	She was washing up *out* in the kitchen
Omission	Circle word/s left out	She was washing (up) in the kitchen
Pause	Stroke, use when reader pauses for more than two seconds	She was washing/up in the kitchen
Repetition	Mark the word/s repeated with a curved line	She was washing up *R* in the kitchen
Correction*	Write in original miscue, then curved line with the letter (c) for self-correction	(c)*had been* (c)*bowl* She was washing up in the kitchen

*Clay (1969) found in her study of beginners that her 'high' progress group not only made fewer mistakes than the 'low' group but also differed in their correction of errors. The 'high' group corrected one in three or four errors in comparison with the 'low' group's error correction rate of one in twenty.

Page No. & line No.	HAPPY TRIO READING SCHEME (pages 90, 91 and 92) Our New Friends Part 1 - 'Puff's Ride.'	NOTES MARTIN

90 01	It was time to feed Puff.	Illustrations:
90 02	So Dick went out for her milk	Dick calling Puff
90 03	~R~ ~a-a~ and began to call the kitten.	with a saucer in his hand.
90 04	"Come, Puff! Come here!"	
90 05	But Puff did not come to	
90 06	get her milk.	
90 07	Then Dick began looking for her.	
90 08	So did Jane.	
91 01	"Here comes a man with a basket	Dick and Jane see
91 02	© ~for-for Mother~ of things for Mother," said Jane.	a man in the distance, wearing
91 03	"Let's ask him to help find Puff."	a white uniform with a peaked cap
91 04	⎰ ("Hello, children," said the man.) *Coughs*	and carrying a box
91 05	"Are you / looking ~R~ for © me?" *and goes back to*	containing what appears to be
91 06	"We are looking for Puff," *discuss line 9104*	flowers.
91 07	said Dick.	
91 08	"Do you / *call* know where she can be?"	
91 09	"No Dick," said the man. _to_	
91 10	"I wish I could help you ^ find her.	
91 11	But I must go back to the shop."	
92 01	Up the street walked ~Bill~ © *Big Ben* Big Bill.	Dick and Jane see a policeman coming
92 02	"What are you doing?" he said.	towards them.
92 03	"Are you looking for me?"	

TEACHER'S NOTES I asked this child more than four questions because his answers were very short, and I wanted, if possible, to encourage him to talk. It can be seen from his answers how much information he had absorbed from the illustrations.

T: What was special about the time of day?
   Dick knew it was an important time.
C: Feeding time.
T: Feeding time for who?
C: Puff.
T: Who is Puff?
C: A cat.
T: Did Puff come when Dick called her?
C: No.
T: What did Dick and Jane do?
C: Look for him - her.
T: Who did they ask to help them?
C: A man - that man - here. (points)
T: I wonder what sort of job this man had?
C: Worked in a shop.
T: What sort of a shop do you think that man worked in?
C: A flower shop, flowers.
T: Why do you think he worked in a flower shop? (Martin
   pointed to the illustration. The man could have been
   carrying a box with two flowering plants.)
   Was this man able to help them?
C: Yes - yes. He found Puff already - I think, I think
   he had.
T: Had he?
C: Yes - look at that in the van - right there.
   (Illustration of Puff riding in a milk float. The man
   with the 'flowers' is wearing the same sort of uniform
   as the milkman!)

NB The confusion over Big Bill. Was he thinking of Big Ben,
the clock or Bill and Ben the flowerpot men?

CA = 7.2 years
RA (Schonell) = 6.0
MA (Goodenough) = 138.

SCHEME Happy Trio (Wheaton)

MISCUES

1 Corrections = 4
2 Substitutions = 5
3 Insertions = 0
4 Omissions = 0

No of words = 124
No of errors = (uncorrected) 1

Word recognition level = $\frac{1}{124}$

Independent Stage = 99%

Comprehending Score = 80%

Left: a teacher's assessment of a child's reading ability. This is the same child, Martin, as in the Schonell test on page 101.

Below: an example of Martin's work

I am grateful to V. Manzi, one of the teachers attending a course at the Centre for the Teaching of Reading, for providing the notes on Martin.

References

BLANTON, W. E., et al., *Measuring reading performances*, Newark, Delaware: International Reading Association, 1974

CLAY, M. M., *Reading: the patterning of complex behaviour*, Heinemann Educational, 1973

FARR, R., *Reading: what can be measured?* Newark, Delaware: International Reading Association, 1970

GOODACRE, E. J., *Hearing children read*, School of Education, University of Reading. Available from the Centre for the Teaching of Reading, 29 Eastern Avenue, Reading. 2nd rev. edn 1974

GOODMAN, K., ed., *Miscue analysis: applications to reading instruction* (ERIC Clearing house on Reading and Communication Skills) Campaign III: National Council of Teachers of English, 1973

GOODMAN, K., 'A linguistic study of cues and miscues in reading', *Elementary English*, 1965, pp. 639–43

MACGINITIE, W. H., ed., *Assessment problems in reading*, Newark, Delaware: International Reading Association, 1973

SMITH, F., *Comprehension and learning – a conceptual framework for teachers*, Holt, Rhinehart and Winston, 1976

Part 4   Resources

by Betty Root, Tutor-in-charge at the Centre for the Teaching of Reading, University of Reading School of Education

Considering that children have been taught to read for centuries, materials designed specifically for this purpose are relatively new. Indeed, reading schemes as we know them today are scarcely more than half a century old, and over these fifty years I can personally register many changes. Little choice existed before the 1940s and probationary teachers entering an infant class for the first time found not only neat piles of dreary books in the cupboards but also a specific syllabus of work indicating exactly how and when to use them. Class reading was certainly dominant, and perhaps some of you can recall the sheer boredom of waiting for your turn or being caught out because you were day-dreaming or had raced ahead and lost the place. Whilst I do not deny that some of the practices of the good old days were educationally sound, nevertheless the present-day situation where the needs of each individual child take precedence over all else, must surely be seen as progress. Unfortunately, many people adopt a narrow stance and can only think of either/or situations. We would do well to recollect and adopt some of the good practice from those formal days and my own personal view would lead me to recall one important factor – teachers knew exactly where they were going.

Somewhere over the past fifty years this notion underlying the education of young children has become submerged amongst the creative writing, early science, language experience and the rest of the new jargon. It is clear that a number of teachers do not have a planned programme and do not keep a clear view ahead. Intuitive teaching there must be, but it is only acceptable to me alongside a sound, comprehensive, organised plan of action. Such a planned programme must essentially arise from discussion involving the whole school staff. Over the last two decades

I can see that many teachers have gone their own way despite the team-teaching boom which has unfortunately not always grown from a natural situation but often has been inflicted on a school by some ambitious adviser.

Repercussions from the *Bullock Report* are understandably slow to permeate the school staffroom, but there is evidence that one major issue is surfacing. Teachers are talking about reorganising the reading and language learning in their schools somewhat along the same lines suggested in part 1, page 18. More than that, teachers are endeavouring to explore further how they can tackle this major task. It is a healthy sign that reading courses offered throughout the United Kingdom, are always generously oversubscribed.

Naturally, as a course provider I would like to think that the quality of reading and language courses is sufficiently high to effect actual change in the classroom. It is not difficult as a lecturer to inspire teachers but it is necessary to go much further than this. Thankfully large numbers of excellent teachers' centres have been established over the past ten years and these provide the meeting ground for teachers to exchange ideas; it is the small working parties established as a result of courses or lectures which will in the end be responsible for true change in attitudes towards language and reading in our schools. Individual teachers are responsible for their own knowledge and surely responsible for ensuring that throughout each school knowledge is shared. Perhaps we have moved too far away from actually teaching and become solely organisers of learning experiences. Both activities are required from all of us.

Finding out about resource material

As well as having a complete understanding of what to plan *for*, it is also essential to know what to plan *with*. Regrettably some teachers are not so well informed and they struggle on, using out of date, often ineffective, resources. A mass of education journals advertise the products of many publishers. Sending away for inspection copies has long been the task of the most dedicated teachers. Whilst this has some advantages, it is not an ideal solution because only part of a whole programme is received and this can be unsatisfactory and misleading. It is though an improvement on purchasing direct from the catalogue, a practice to be strongly discouraged.

Fortuitously, as more materials have become available, so too has the evidence of better, more frequent and widespread exhibitions. Several hundred varied teachers' centres scattered throughout the country help enormously to disseminate information throughout the teaching profession. Some teachers' centres have excellent reading resource areas, though not all of them can offer specific advice in the area of reading and language. Reading centres have been established in many authorities and colleges of education; these usually provide expert help and direction around the resources. The Centre for the Teaching of Reading, University of Reading, has a permanent exhibition of *every* publication concerning reading and language at all levels. This display is open to everyone and is not restricted to professionals in the locality. Here visitors are able to obtain help if required, or just browse. A postal and telephone information service is also offered.

With the steady growth of centres it is not too difficult for most teachers to reach exhibitions at regular intervals. By seeing and studying a wide selection of resources, confident decisions can be made and money spent wisely. The important point for a teacher to remember is – decide for yourself.

Perhaps these decisions can be made less arduous by consulting some of the excellent advice made available through a selection of books. Almost all such publications require constant updating if they are to be of any value. The following meet this requirement and are most useful.

The A–Z of reading
Publisher: National Association of Remedial Education (NARE), 4 Old Croft Road, Walton-on-the-Hill, Stafford.

This slim book lists several hundred books and gives an assessment of the readability level based on the Spache Readability Test. The books listed cover infant, junior and secondary, though in the latter section titles are restricted to those most suited to the slower readers.

A classroom index of phonic resources
Publisher: NARE (as above).

Teachers are finding this publication an enormous help. It is concerned with resources available for helping with the teaching of phonic skills. Each skill – initial consonants, short and long vowels, digraphs, etc., is given a separate page and a comprehensive list of where to find exercises and/or activities for giving practice in that particular element. Thus children can be given practice in a variety of ways and this is so important to ensure a transfer of learning.

Basic reading schemes
Publisher: National Book League, 7 Albemarle Street, London W1X 4BB.

This small book adequately describes many popular reading schemes. It is worth noting that the NBL publishes several similar booklets which include

Books for the teachers of backward children

Teaching reading

English for immigrant children

Starting point (Books for Adult New Readers)

Six reading schemes by D. Latham
Publisher: Cambridge Institute of Education.

This book describes in detail six reading schemes, their emphasis and interchangeability. Information is provided on vocabulary load and phonic difficulty. The six schemes are *Beacon, Happy trio, Happy venture, Janet and John, Through the rainbow, Time for reading*. It is hoped that a similar piece of work will be carried out with more up to date schemes.

Reading schemes
Publisher: West Sussex Education Department.

Qualitative description of 85 reading schemes and series. Charts giving reading and interest age are also included. West Sussex also publish other booklets, including *Phonics and teaching non readers*.

Learning to read by B. Root
Publisher: Centre for the Teaching of Reading University of Reading (rev. edn 1976).

This publication catalogues almost all the books available. It gives particulars of price, content and publisher of books for early readers, primary schemes, reluctant readers, immigrant readers. This publication is updated each year.

Individualised reading
Publisher: Centre for the Teaching of Reading, University of Reading.
This book suggests a colour coding system for a number of schemes and supplementary readers. It is intended to be a guide for schools

not using one basic scheme. Several hundred books have been grouped into 13 stages. This publication is updated twice each year.

Cliff Moon, the author, has also helped to compile comparative lists of Young Puffins to enable teachers to colour code *all* books in the classroom. These lists are available from Penguin Books Ltd.

What kind of information is available in your school about the range and variety of published resource material?

Choosing books

Fortunately, teachers in this country do have the freedom of choice concerning the books used in their school. It has never been my philosophy to make decisions for teachers, rather to set out the choice available. Individuals do have varying opinions about books and I feel that no one has the authority to dictate choice. Even so, it is worth considering the criteria essential to selection.

● However simple, you must read the books yourself. Perhaps this is stating the obvious, though I think not.

● Decide if the book is worth reading; usually, reading it aloud will help you to find out if the language flows and if an element of suspense is present.

● If the book is intended as an early reader, does the text relate to the illustration? Never forget that young children do rely heavily on reading the picture. It is unfair to mislead children when it is comparatively simple to eliminate such an error.

● Study the size of print, it is the spacing of words on a page which effects clarity. Avoid

Fred and Emma gave the birds and the rabbits some of their sandwiches.

One day their mummy and daddy said it was time to go home. Fred and Emma had had such fun that the time had flown by very quickly. They were sad that their wonderful holiday had come to an end.

In the morning they said:

"Mother, we are going to show the giant cat that he is not the king of the forest. You must help us. If he comes back, do not tell him that you have two sons. Tell him you have only one."

So that day Carlo went out as usual with his bow and

books where black print is placed on a coloured ground.

● Look at the cultural bias of the book and when doing so remember the children who will be reading it.

● Is the readability level suggested by the publisher realistic? Often this is not so. Remember that readability formula are seldom suitable for very early readers.

● The teacher's manual will often give you information about the progressive element built into the text. Make sure you are familiar with the vocabulary load so that you understand the task you set the child and appreciate the amount of support material he is likely to require for consolidation.

● Try to avoid books which use contrived and unnatural language. Children are anxious to read and bring all their intelligence to bear when tackling the initial task. Some of their pronouncements will be guessing, but if the text has been written thoughtfully children will be able to 'detect sequential probability in the linguistic structure'. (*Language for life.*)

● Finally, continually remind yourself that it is the *children's* opinions which really matter. A wide selection of books must be available to suit the individual needs of your children. Insist that one basic reading scheme, however good, is just not enough.

What criteria do you use when deciding on resource material? Which of the above criteria do you rate most important?

Reading schemes and supplementary readers

In the past there has been an inherent weakness in reading schemes which has led both teachers and children to think of them as something different and apart from 'real books'. What a ridiculous division it is; is there any sign that a merger is taking place? I think so. Several of the newer schemes are represented on the shelves of the local libraries, this is an indication that the quality of such books has improved much beyond the 'Go Tim go, go up up up.' Librarians, though, tell me that it is sometimes difficult to resist the demands made by parents for *Janet and John* and the like to be available on loan. Parental involvement we do need, but not in this way.

Since not all are widely known, it is worth commenting on some of the newer schemes, remembering that a scheme consists of a series of graded readers with support materials and a teacher's handbook. With this definition in mind, 28 schemes are available, almost 50% of these were published prior to 1950. For the purpose of this handbook only the more recent ones will be discussed, perhaps with one exception. Mention must be made of the *Beacon* scheme since it has survived 54 long years, and parts of which are still widely used in primary schools. I suspect that those teachers using *Little Chick-chick* as a starting point with small children are a dying race, but so many teachers agree with me that the last four books of the *Beacon* scheme contain traditional stories extremely well told, and although they may not have glossy covers and eye-catching illustrations, nevertheless the literary content is excellent. It is easy to get our priorities wrong, and some less responsible publishers believe that a good glossy cover will sell anything; let us hope that such publishers go bankrupt!

the driver is reading
in the lorry.

12

Mother said, "Look, Susan.

This mitten is gone.

There is no mitten here."

Susan said, "Where did it go?

I will have to find it.

Where will I look?"

Breakthrough to literacy
by D. Mackay, B. Thompson, and P. Schaub
Publisher: Longman

Teacher's manual
My sentence maker
Pupil's sentence maker folder
Pupil's plastic stand
Project folder
My first word book
Teacher's sentence maker, including inserts and
  stand
Magnetic board pack
Breakthrough to literacy filmstrip, with teacher's
  notes
First word maker
Teacher's first word maker
My word maker (original version) (additional
  and replacement letters and words are available)
Breakthrough books, 4 books to each set
  Yellow sets A, B, C, D, E
  Red sets A, B, C, D, E, Jokers
  Blue sets, A, B
  Green sets A, B, C (same reading level as red
    sets, stories more sophisticated, suitable for
    slow learners)
2 Big breakthrough books
'Sally go round the sun' record
'Sally go round the sun' cards
Breakthrough poetry, 4 books
Lollipops

This is not strictly a scheme and was never
intended to be so, but it would be impossible
to leave it out of any discussion concerned
with ways of helping children to read.
Breakthrough was launched with waving
banners six years ago. The generous advanced
publicity misled many people into believing
that all the answers had been found; to be
fair, the authors of this extensive work had
never made such claims. Despite some initial
disappointments from over-optimistic teachers,
Breakthrough now contributes to our infant
schools a language experience approach
alongside other ways of teaching reading. One
rarely hears about disappointment now, and
the excellent handbook has enabled teachers
to understand in greater depth the rationale
behind this project. New materials have been
added over the years and an independent
evaluation was made by Jessie Reid in 1974,
published by Longman.

Observing in many schools I have come to
the conclusion that working with *Breakthrough*
has led many teachers to develop their own
innovations in teaching reading. This indicates
to me the quality of the basic ideas inherent
in the original materials.

Dominoes
by D. Glynn. Publisher: Oliver and Boyd
Picture books – 2 sets of 4 books
Stages 1 and 2 (6 books in each Stage)
Stage 3 (6 books)
Stage 4 (6 books)
Stage 5 (6 books)
Stage 6 (in preparation)
Teacher's guide
Pictorial discussion book
Flash cards (nouns) (stage 1)
Flash cards (verbs) (stage 1)
Practice folders (stage 1 and stage 2)
Practice holders (stage 3)
Domino games (stage 1 and 2)
Dominoes glove puppets (stage 1 and 2)
Filmstrips (stage 1 and 2)
Stage 1 (6 books) ⎫ *Dominoes extras*
Stage 2 (6 books) ⎭
Dominoes read, write and colour
My alphabet book

we eat at school.

2

we eat school dinners.

3

This scheme, in six stages, enjoys popularity in many schools. Because the first books are all school based rather than home based, it is particularly useful for immigrant children and those who live in unenviable surroundings. All can identify with the school situation; like *Through the rainbow*, the earlier books do not have original illustrations but rely on colour photography. The idea is excellent but in practice the final product can be a little confusing. There is so much going on in the pictures it becomes difficult for a child to extract the most important happening and so relate to illustration. Various support materials extend the books. There are also plastic hand puppets which are disappointing.

Gay way by E. R. Boyce

Publisher Macmillan

Teaching pictures and introductory reading
Vocabulary
Picture dictionary
Picture dictionary workbooks (4)
Rhyme book
Nursery rhyme pictures
Song book
6 basic readers
Supplementary readers (8 for each basic reader)
Introductory pictures
Auxiliary readers (18 – some in i.t.a.)

Briefly, it is worth noting that this scheme has a more contrived language because of its phonic constrictions. Remembering that children learn in different ways, I believe books of this kind should be available in the classroom. The newer story books added to this scheme in recent years are highly recommended.

A completely revised version of *Gayway* is to be published shortly.

The language project
Consultant: Dr Joyce Morris, Publisher: Macmillan

Level 0 – pre-literacy, 13 titles
Level 0–1 – alphabet
  Introductory books (5)
  Group 1 – 8 books
  Group 2 – 7 books
Level 1 – basic language structures – 1
  (12 titles)
Level 2 – basic language structures – 2 (8 titles)
Level 3 – basic language structures – 3 (2 titles)
Level 4 – language guides
  Language in action resource book
  Language in action resource book – supplement
  Background book
  Creative writing
  The new media challenge
  Literacy: Language experience approaches
  Books and the under-sixes

This is another programme which enjoyed enormous pre-publication publicity. Not surprising, since it is the brainchild of a well respected international figure in the field of reading, Dr Joyce Morris. *The language project* is the work of a team of experts and very much thought has been given to a different way of looking at early reading. The programme is comprehensive and based on an analysis of the constituent parts of our language. All teachers using this material should first of all read the two resource books and, if possible,

the other helpful books which accompany the programme. Without background knowledge it would be impossible to use this extensive material to the best advantage. Not all the children's books are available yet, but already teachers find the earlier books very helpful. All are beautifully produced and satisfying to handle.

Laugh and learn by Terry Hall
Publisher: Alexander

Basic books (6)
Supplementary readers (18)

Terry Hall, the author of these books is a well known television personality who entertains children with a ventriloquist's dummy called Lenny the Lion. This series sets out initially to entertain, to make reading content amusing through cartoon-like illustrations and succinct text. For these reasons the books are very different from other schemes. On first inspection there are some teachers who would object to the comic-like figures and the slap-stick type humour contained in *Laugh and learn*. Nevertheless it must be remembered that a great number of our children arrive at school with a negligible amount of experience as far as story-telling is concerned. Not a few of these children have drawn on comics for their pleasures. *Laugh and learn* is proving to be extremely successful as 'bridger' books. I've received repeated reports concerning their attractiveness to children. We would do well to remind ourselves that we select books for the children's pleasure as well as our own. There is no doubt that our personal attitudes often require careful examination.

Sammy skates ever so fast
all over the town.
But he goes so fast
he can not stop.
He is such a silly seal
to skate so fast.

15

Link-up by J. Read and J. Low
Publisher: Holmes McDougall

8 Trailer books
8 Link-up reading books
8 Build-up books
Laminated pictures with 'limpet' words, set of 2
Lotto cards with cut-out words, set of 6
Laminated 'limpet' card, with self-stick words
 and letters
3 Sets draw and write cards (10 per set)
Teacher's manual

At the present time *Link-up* has a limited
amount of material, only 24 books are available;
it is hoped more of similar quality will be
added. Already many schools use this material
with great enthusiasm. It is especially suited
to schools in urban surroundings with a
multi-racial intake, but by no means need be
restricted to such areas. The beginning stages
incorporate the environmental words which
the children meet in their everyday life. The
two large attractive posters have these
everyday sight words in cellograph which are
placed in position by the children, and provide
a change from the evergreen flash cards.

Look I'm reading
by S. H. Haskell and M. E. Paul
Publisher: ESA (Creative Learning)

Pre-scheme: Training in basic cognitive skills,
 28 booklets, Training in basic motor skills
 8 books – Books 1–7, Book 8
 Handbook
Phase 1: Unit 1 – 44 alphabet cards in box
  Unit 2 – 440 picture and word cards in
   44 envelopes and a strong box
  Unit 3 – 20 window books in box
  Unit 4 – 5 alphabet children's books
  Unit 5 – 10 sentence books

Phase 2: 10 story books
 Teacher's handbook
 Starter pack, includes units 1–3 and handbook
 Lotto game, 6 boards and 120 word cards, boxed

This extensive programme is being published
in several stages over a period of time. It is
the only scheme in this country to include a
total training pack for basic motor and
cognitive skills. A pack which can, of course, be
used independently. Phase 1 of this scheme is
concerned with phonic skills and does not
have story books but a variety of activities.
Phase 2 is composed of books but they are not
essentially story books, but books to practice
the phonic skills acquired. All the material is
well produced.

One, two, three and away!
by S. K. McCullagh, Publisher: Hart-Davis
Introductory readers A–D
Platform readers A–D
Platform readers level 1 (6)
Books 1–4A (8 books)
Platform readers level 2 (6 books)
Books 5–8
Platform readers level 3 (6 books)
Books 9–12
Alphabet book
Story people (wooden figures of main characters)
Word cards, 2 sets
Question cards
Set of 5 posters
Teacher's handbook
In preparation – 5 work books and other materials

S. K. McCullagh, the author of this scheme is,
without doubt, held in high esteem by
countless teachers. Some do not know her
name but all faces light up when you mention

Pirates. One, two, three and away! is intended for young children just beginning to read. Few people can write within the restrictions of a controlled vocabulary and the characters they draw usually seem lifeless. Not so the inhabitants of the *Village with three corners*. All are lively and have something to give and say, 38 books relate their adventures. Interesting and unusual support material complete a satisfying total programme. Two minor comments: the type face of the flash cards is not always the same as in the books, children get confused, especially with the 't'. It is important to remember that children who have been deprived of substantial story experiences at home find it less easy to enter into the imaginative stories of *One, two, three and away!* Such children do desperately need to be immersed in endless story-telling during their early days in school.

Read systems (Commonwealth)
Publisher: Scott-Foresman

6 levels, each level includes:
Teacher's resource book
Teacher's read aloud library
Pupil's books (packages of between 4 to 9 books)
Study books
Spirit masters
Magnetic board and pieces.

A relatively new American scheme which has been anglicised by Keith Gardner for the UK market. Because of its American origins you would expect lavish pre-reading materials and substantial handbooks. These you have as well as the six different levels of readers. Unlike many of our schemes *Read systems* is not based on a family theme and seems therefore very fresh and varied. The books are most attractively produced and contain a mixture of stories and information. To take the place of expendable work-books there are books of spirit masters which enable teachers to produce their own work sheets most economically. In America this series extends right through the primary levels, so it is to be hoped that the advanced levels will be edited for sale in this country.

Schools using this material are stimulated and encouraged by the results they are obtaining. Surprisingly enough the books are not too expensive.

Sparks by R. M. Fisher and others
Publisher: Blackie

Teacher's guide
Stage one red
  12 pre-readers
Teacher's story book
Concertina book

Stage two blue
  8 family booklets
  Sentence matching cards (72)
  Family shaped books (4)
  Matching word cards (4 sets)
Stage three green
  16 books
Stage four yellow
  4 books
Stage five pink
  4 books
Stage six purple
  8 books
Sparks bookshelf levels one and two
  16 books

This scheme is particularly suited to children living in urban areas. All the books are attractively produced and have an air of realism about them. The stories, especially at level 6, are particularly good. Since the vocabulary grading is somewhat steep, the books should be supported by some imaginative material for consolidation and reinforcement. The slim handbook is highly recommended and does include a few ideas for games and activities. More recently *Sparks bookshelf* has been added, in all this makes an attractive proposition for many of our children.

Time for reading by C. Obrist and P. Pickard
Publisher: Ginn

Stage 1: The picture book stage
Stage 2: The Cherry family
  8 quickies
Stage 3: Penny's birthday
  Story books 1–6
Stage 4: Penny at school
  Story books 7–12
Stories for today
  6 books

Full support materials for stages 1–4
Stage 5: The bread and butter house
Stage 6: The little wooden horse
Stage 7: The dancing harp
Work cards for stages 5, 6 and 7
2 work books for use at home
Teacher's manual
Time for sounds (introduction to phonic work)
   4 books
Time for stories
   6 books

This scheme was first introduced 12 years ago and seems best suited to a good middle-class area. Some of the books have become a little dated, but this is inevitable. Over the years a variety of new material has been added so the total programme is very substantial and does extend into the junior age range. As well as over 40 books, the scheme also includes games, work books and wall pictures. More recently a story cassette and spirit masters for outline pictures have been introduced and the hitherto excellent handbook rewritten in the light of all the new materials included in the scheme. Here is an author, Celia Obrist, aware of the need to approach reading in a multi-sensorial way. It is good to see a well established scheme continuing to grow.

How many of these schemes are you familiar with?

From these descriptions of just eleven major reading programmes you can decude that all schemes are not dull and boring. Used imaginatively there is no doubt that schemes contribute an essential role in the reading programmes of many schools. It is not in any way essential to use a reading scheme. Some teachers rely totally on the children's own experiences and the happenings in school to provide individual personalised books for each child. The role of the teacher cannot be over-emphasised, it is the teacher who can make effective or indifferent use of books. It is vital not only to teach reading but to make readers.

Which schemes do you think would help those children described in part 1, pages 30 and 37?

Of the children in your class, which find the schemes you use adequate? Of those who are experiencing difficulties, do you think any of them would benefit from using some alternative material listed above?

A selection of books for older, reluctant readers

Some children do not learn to read easily but it is quite wrong to label them 'backward'. If they require more help over a longer period of time care must be taken to ensure that the organisation of reading in the school allows this to happen. Most children respond to individual help from the classroom teacher and only a few require specialised instruction away from their normal environment. If children have reached the junior or middle school with little reading ability, it is unfair to present them with infant books. There is a wealth of material written for a higher interest level with a careful use of vocabulary and sentence structure. Remember that the major obstacle to overcome with reluctant readers is one of motivation. It is so vital to provide a wide selection of story and information books so that each child can choose according to his own interests. Here are some suggestions.

Approach trend – Ginn
Adventures in space – Hart-Davis

Canal Street – Nelson

Cowboy Sam – E. J. Arnold

Griffin and dragon stories – E. J. Arnold

Help – Nelson

Inswingers – Hulton

Pop swingers – Hulton

Jim Hunter – Methuen

Racing to read – E. J. Arnold

Rescue stories – Ginn

Star family – E. J. Arnold

A list of supplementary and extension readers

It is totally impossible to include all those available. Exclusion from this list does not infer disapproval.

Early readers:

Beginner books – Collins

Beginning beginner books – Collins

Beginning to read – Benn

Books without words – Black

Dinosaur books – Dinosaur

Leading to reading – G. P. Alexander

Olga da polga – Kestrel

See how it grows – Macmillan

Seven silly stories – Longman

Stories to start with – Hart-Davis

Tell-a-tale – Macdonald

Zero books – Macdonald

Tarzan tortoise – Longman

This is the way I go – Longman

Talk-rounders – Holmes McDougall

Trug books – Oliver and Boyd

Extension readers:

Bangers and mash – Longman

Beanstalk books – Nelson Young World

Cheshire cats – Ginn

Enjoy reading – Chambers

First and second folk tales – Hart-Davis

Flightpath to reading – E. J. Arnold

Grasshopper – Abelard-Schuman

Green grass books – Heinemann

Monster books – Longman

Nippers and Little nippers – Macmillan

Pleasure in reading – Longman

Read by reading – Longman

Read for fun – Burke

Red apple – Heinemann

Story house – OUP

For full details of all the books and materials mentioned in this chapter, see *Learning to read*, a catalogue of books for all ages and stages, published by Centre for the Teaching of Reading.

Non-book resources for reading

Whilst it would be totally irresponsible to underestimate the importance of books and their central role in the teaching of reading to young children, nevertheless it must be recognised that non-book material has a part to play. The extent of this contribution varies with each individual child, but it is more likely that the slower and reluctant readers, perhaps those too who lack motivation, will require more help of this nature.

Colour coding resource materials will enable you, as teachers, to provide the correct level and content of material for each individual child. If you require help in identifying the levels of games, cassettes, reading laboratories etc., Bridie Raban of Bristol Reading Centre has carried out considerable research in this area. It can be found in two books:

A question of reading

by B. Raban and C. Moon
Publisher: Ward Lock

Reading skill acquisition

by B. Raban. Publisher: Centre for the Teaching of Reading, University of Reading School of Education.

Reading games and general activities

It is important to remember that children require many opportunities to practice their newly acquired skills. Knowledge of words is in the first instance usually taught within the context of a meaningful sentence. Knowledge of building new words, blending sounds together, is usually taught orally by the teacher. In order that such knowledge is reinforced and consolidated, children need to transfer their learning to many other situations. It is a mistake to assume that because a child can read particular words which appear on a certain page and under a certain picture, he can then recognise the word elsewhere. Reading games and activities help enormously in this sphere of transferred learning. Dull repetition in the text of the books can be eliminated if the teacher has in her overall planning allowed for a variety of support material. Some of this material is as dreary as the repetitive text. Idly matching pictures and words is a useless occupation. In order to motivate children there must be inbuilt purposeful activity. Group reading games provide just this.

These are the criteria I use in assessing games:

● Is the game an extension of the child's reading? Does it provide suitable reinforcement?

● Is it self-corrective, and are the correct responses immediately rewarded?

● Is the activity colour coded, to facilitate easy matching with the child's stage of development.

● Is each part of the game identifiable so that when found on the floor it can be returned, by the child, to the correct storage box?

Do the games and activities you use in your classroom match up well to these criteria?

Published games are not numerous but those listed below have been well reviewed over the past few years. It is impossible to present a very comprehensive list here, and again exclusion does not in any way suggest disapproval.

Word and picture plaques (family transport, food, alphabet, etc. Very well made) – E. J. Arnold

Locking letters – Abbatt

Animal shuffle book – ESA

Story shuffle book – ESA

Self-checking comprehension cards – Galt

Sound links – Galt

Word patterns – Galt

Colour learning game – Galt

Say what you see – Galt

Betty Root reading games – Good reading

Bear game   ⎫
Spin and win   ⎬ Games for
Elephant game   ⎬ whole word
Score a goal   ⎭ recognition

Spot the crocodile   ⎫
Rabbit game   ⎬ Games for
Turn the wheel   ⎬ phonic
Fish game   ⎭ practice

Betty Root card games – Hart-Davis

Stott programmed reading kit – Holmes
McDougall
30 carefully graded series of games with a
definite phonic approach

Lingo – Hope
a substantial bingo-type game for recognising
letters and groups of letters

Reading games – Macmillan
a kit containing 20 base boards and all
additional material required to play them.

These games are not self-corrective but are
excellent for teacher-supervised groups

Roll-a-story – Penguin
a fun game for children to make their own
amusing sentences

Philip and Tacey produce a very large number
of reading activities. They are too numerous to
list here, but each item is described in detail
in the catalogue.

Programmed kits

Since this chapter is concerned with resources
for reading it would be wrong to omit mention
of the various programmed kits which have
increased considerably over the past few years.
Before listing them I believe a word of caution is
justified. Kits usually come in easily stored and
portable boxes and some teachers view these
packages as a panacea and use them relentlessly
without any consideration of the global needs
of children learning to read. This misuse has,
in some respects, damaged the image of such

kits, so that they are unreservedly dismissed. Now this is unfortunate because, used intelligently and selectively, as part of a total programme, individual kits can prove enormously helpful, especially where there is a wide range of children's ability and teaching ability too!

Reading Laboratories are available from:
SRA – Laboratories for many levels from 6–10.
Ward Lock – produce three laboratories 6–13.
Longman – produce *Reading routes* 7–12.

Do you use any programmed kits? Do you feel that these dangers are real ones?

Audio and visual materials

Expensive educational equipment has proliferated in the past decade. There seems some danger that we have measured educational advance only in terms of money spent and not by actual performance. So little research has been published on the true effects of introducing 'machines' into the classroom. Are such machines indispensable? The answer has to be no, but this does not mean to say that machines have no value. Since this is a technological age I believe we should accept the advantages but with caution. Not all teachers have a flair for devising programmes and not all machines have suitable flexible software. Machines though can give *individual* help when the teacher's time has to be divided amongst so many children. It is an advantage if the software can be produced by teachers as well as being produced by publishers. All the following meet this requirement.

Audio page – E. J. Arnold

Each work sheet has a magnetic backing for a 4-minute recording. The writing side can be typed on, or drawings can be stuck on.

Prepared software includes phonic programmes, very early sight vocabulary and rhyming work, reasoning, science, etc.

Language master – Bell and Howell

This machine works with cards which have a two-track tape at the bottom for teacher and child voices. A child reads and records, then switches over to hear the teacher, thus obtaining instant correction. Software includes *word study, word blending, find the word*, and many others.
The *Language master* has been well tested in schools of all kinds; there has been time for the novelty to wear off and it is proving to be very effective.

Card reader – Rank Audio Visual

This is very similar to the *Language master*. The software is interchangeable.

Filmstrip and slide viewers

A variety of these are available and several publishers produce good visual material:

Educational Productions

Ladybird Books Ltd

Slide Centre Ltd

Weston Woods Studios Ltd

The latter produce a variety of excellent film strips, especially suited to the reading situation.

Do you use audio visual equipment? Do you produce your own software-worksheets, cards, etc.?

Cassette tape recorders

These have become most popular in all schools. Not surprising since they are both cheap and portable. Operation is simple, so that most teachers can make their own tapes. The children have no trouble, and older children in the school enjoy making tapes for the younger ones. A very wide selection of tapes is available but quality and length varies. The following have proved to be reliable and useful:

Sounds lotto – E. J. Arnold

Griffin & pirate dramatic stories – E. J. Arnold

Listening to sounds (phonic work) – E. J. Arnold

Storytellers – Drake Educational

Gateway stories – Gateway Educational

Listening and reading – Penguin Educational

Time for reading – Ginn

We can read – Hodder and Stoughton

Pictures in sound – Remedial Supply Association

Cassette/books – Scholastic

Listening laboratories – SRA

Several kits at different levels, each having cassettes and work books. These kits are for language enrichment and develop auditory skills.

Men of the west – Good reading

This is a complete literacy programme, suitable for children who have not acquired any reading skills. Because of its wide ranging cowboy and indian content, it will appeal to older reluctant readers. 10 cassettes, story cards and a wide variety of work sheets and games all combine to make this a very attractive kit for children of all abilities.

Language development materials

The effects of language deprivation on children have been widely discussed and research during the past few years. It is not surprising that publishers are now providing a variety of language stimulus resources. Whilst many teachers will continue to create their own ways of encouraging children to use the language, others will find some of the commercially produced material an invaluable help in the classroom. Often the use of such material will greatly inspire teachers to extend the programme to suit the needs of her particular children.

Living language – Macmillan

A plastic wall-hanging holder containing two copies each of six books and sets of photographs and word cards to match books.

Concept 7–9 – E. J. Arnold

A course developed by Schools Council designed for children of 7–9. The course is divided into four units.

Listening with understanding
Concept building
Communication
Dialect

Language development pack – E. J. Arnold

Two cassettes and spirit masters provide listening activities.

Language resource pack – E. J. Arnold

Five posters, cassette with five stories; figures and vehicles to be used on background.

Talking shop – E. J. Arnold

Large board with shop windows. Cassette tells children to place cards in windows.

Tell tales – Evans

Cards in display unit (4 in sequence).
Teacher's book
Children tell the story.

Jim's people – Hart-Davis

Three sets.
Bold pictures designed to stimulate language.

Goal – Learning Development Aids

An extensive kit with many component parts.

Language activities kit – Scott-Foresman

A very useful series of activities and excellent manual.

Radio and television

In recent years radio and television have increased provision for the primary schools especially in the important areas of reading and language. At one time many educationists considered that broadcast programmes were 'time fillers'. If it was so then, I do not consider that this is the situation now. The excellent teacher's notes which accompany the lessons facilitate much more effective follow-up plans. If teachers do not use these notes they need to rethink their attitudes. Not everyone is aware of the wealth of material available from the BBC; records and cassettes of previously broadcast material, for example. It could be argued, and rightly so, that it is impossible to segregate any programmes from reading and language but in order to reduce the list, I mention only those series whose aim is specifically related to reading and language. It is essential and fruitful to look carefully at the *Annual Programmes* published by the BBC and IBA.

Current Programmes for primary schools

Television:

You and Me
Pre-school children watch this *with* adults

Words and Pictures
For children in the early stages of reading.

Look and Read
Highly motivating for older children still struggling with reading.

The Electric Company
Slick American series suitable for all young children and especially the language-disadvantaged in the 9–14 age group.

Radio:

Listening and Reading
Three separate broadcasts for older infants, 8 year olds and 11–13 year olds. Readings of exciting books. Children follow the text in books provided by the BBC to go with these programmes.

Let's Join In
Dramatised stories for young children.

Poetry Corner
Poems, humorous and otherwise for infants.

Wordplay
To encourage the spoken language development of 8–12 year olds.

Stories and Rhymes
Especially for children from 7–9.

Local Radio:
It would be impossible to list the current provision made by BBC local radio stations as a contribution towards language education in schools. Many of the series have proved themselves highly useful and very popular. You can get details from your local radio station.

Poscript

Most schools do have a generous amount of resources; make certain that you are aware of all the books and materials available for use. Make certain too that all resources are classified and accessible to the right children at the right time.

A confused classroom is an indication of confused teaching.

Appendix 1   Annotated bibliography
compiled by Dr Elizabeth Goodacre

There are many interesting American texts, but these are not always easily available in this country, so the following list has been confined to titles published in this country. Various journals also often publish articles of interest but to include these would have lengthened the list. The Centre for the Teaching of Reading (University of Reading) produces an annual review *Reading research*, which lists and summarises such articles. These annual reviews are a useful source of further reading on specific topics of interest.

ASHWORTH, E. *Language in the junior school* Edward Arnold, Exploring Language Study Series, 1973. Examines ideas about language and how it should be used, and includes chapters on the stages of reading and writing and how teachers can develop literacy skills in the junior school.

BBC PUBLICATIONS *Words and pictures* Teachers' notes to the Series, 1975/76. Suggested activities as follow-up work to the television programmes, which include various reading aids and games related to phonic and vocabulary work.

CHAMBERS, A. *Introducing books to children* Heinemann Educational, 1973. Chapters on story-telling and reading aloud to children, ways of encouraging book ownership among children, and how to encourage young readers to become more selective once they are reading for pleasure. Chs 4, 6 and 10 in particular.

CLAY, M. M. *Reading: the patterning of complex behaviour* Heinemann Educational, 1973. Emphasises the importance of reading 'models' in the young child's environment, directional learning and concepts of print involved in early reading, types of mistakes made and correction rates in reading aloud. Chs 4–7, 10, 12–13.

CLAY, M. M. *What did I write?* Heinemann Educational 1976. Examines young children's efforts at learning to write, explaining how they indicate different stages in acquiring mastery of the skill and provides valuable insights into the relationship between learning to write and the reading process. A short book, delightfully illustrated with examples of children's work.

D'ARCY, P. *Reading for meaning* Volume I *Learning to read*, Hutchinson Educational for the Schools Council (2 volumes), 1973. Chapters on pre-reading period, reading readiness, factors involved in learning to read, teaching methods and techniques such as colour codes and use of audio visual aids, use of reading schemes and alternatives such as Breakthrough and Stott's materials. Fifteen appendices include the findings of important research, lists of books suitable for children, check lists, etc.

DEAN, J. and NICHOLS, R. *Framework for reading* and *Check lists: framework for reading* Evans Bros, 1974. An analysis of the skills and knowledge needed for reading, with suggestions for their development in young children. Also includes examples of suitable check lists which can be used for structuring teachers' observations. These are available separately as printed spirit duplicating masters.

DEPARTMENT OF EDUCATION AND SCIENCE, *A language for life* (*The Bullock Report*) Report of the Committee of Inquiry appointed by the Secretary of State for Education and Science under the Chairmanship of Sir Alan Bullock. Her Majesty's Stationery Office, 1975. Chs 2 and 3 (testing); all of Part 2 and 3 (Chs 4–9); Ch. 10 pages 141–56 (on talking and listening); Ch. 11 pages 167–9, 181–3 (written language including spelling); Ch. 13

(organisation); Part 6 (reading and language difficulties).

DOWNING, J. and THACKRAY, D. *Reading readiness* Hodder and Stoughton, second edn., 1975. A UKRA monograph, which defines and traces the evolution of the concept of reading readiness, and summarises the findings from research regarding the relationship between readiness and physiological, environmental, emotional and intellectual factors. Also discusses the effectiveness of readiness training.

FISHER, M. *Matters of fact: aspects of non-fiction for children*, Brockhampton Press, 1972. An attempt by the author of *Intent upon reading* (which critically reviewed children's fiction) to establish standards for assessing the suitability of information books for young readers. Considers not only accuracy, readability, design and illustrations but also suitability in relation to children's cognitive development of individual titles on themes often used in project work in the primary school.

GAHAGAN, D. M. and G. A., *Talk reform – explorations in language for infant school children*, Routledge and Kegan Paul, n.e. 1972. Chs 3 and 4 deal respectively with the role and function of questions, and games and activities for developing auditory discrimination improving attention and encouraging the use of different language forms.

GILLHAM, W. E. C. *Teaching a child to read* Hodder and Stoughton, 1974. A very short book which could safely be recommended to parents as it places great emphasis upon the need for praise and encouragement of pupils who may be slow to start to learn to read. Programme starts with making the pupil's own reading book based on his or her interests and own language patterns, and includes details of systematic phonic work.

GODDARD, N. *Literacy: language – experience approaches* (A language project language guide), Macmillan, 1974. Describes the rationale of language-experience approaches and compares them to other learning to read approaches. Cites examples of successful practice in schools, and describes how three teachers encouraged each in their own way, children to develop their literacy skills by means of this approach.

GOODACRE, E. J. *Children and learning to read* Routledge and Kegan Paul, 1971. An account of the psychological and perceptual processes involved in the early stages of learning to read, relating these to Piagian ideas on child development. Chs 5 and 6 on visual and auditory development in relation to learning to read.

HOOTON, M., *The First reading and writing book* – A handbook for teachers and parents to use with children, Shepheard-Walwyn, 1976. A systematic introduction to the beginning stages of reading and writing, which includes patterns for making teaching aids, exercises and games; also templates of the letters of the alphabet used for teaching their differing and distinctive shape characteristics.

JOHNSON, T. D. *Reading: teaching and learning* Macmillan Education, 1973. Readable introduction dealing with methods, materials, grouping and assessment. Chapters on beginning stages but also development of the skill by the use of coordinated questions, book reviews, graded reading materials. Appendix includes a worked example of how to use the Fry readability formula.

LANSDOWN, R. R. *Reading: teaching and learning* Pitman, 1974. Ch. 4 'Reading yesterday', an interesting history of literacy and Chapter 6 'Reading today' which analyses the tasks facing the teacher of young readers and suggests activities, games and apparatus which may be of practical help.

MCCULLAGH, S. K. *Into new worlds* Hart-Davis Educational, 1974. Written by a well-known writer of children's reading books explains the main elements of a reading programme which makes extensive use of children's interests and actively encourages their imaginative powers. Very good on the early stages and also on how to help the late starter.

MCKEARN, P. *Reading: a basic guide for parents and teachers* Routledge and Kegan Paul, 1974. Written by a nursery and infant inspector, this book deals with language development, reading readiness, children's familiarity with symbols, visual and auditory discrimination, the main teaching methods and techniques in literacy development.

MCKENZIE, M. and KERNIG, W., *The challenge of informal education* – Extending young children's learning in the open classroom, Darton, Longman and Todd, 1975. Includes a chapter on 'Language and Learning' (pp. 115–35) and in Ch. 6 'Evaluative Learning' pages 143–55 deals with the assessment of growth in literacy. This includes an explanation of Hunt's T-Unit technique for observing the qualitative aspects of children's oral and written language, reference to Goodman's miscue analysis, and examples of detailed record keeping of pupils' literacy development in this type of school organisation.

MELNIK, A. and MERRITT, J. eds *Reading! today and tomorrow* and *The reading curriculum*, Hodder and Stoughton, 1972. Two of three text books produced for the Open University Course on Reading Development, to provide a broad overview of the field of reading, a variety of views on the nature of the reading process and

a review of the various factors involved in reading development. Material in the books comes from papers published in academic journals, conference proceedings, and extracts from books dealing with reading. Part I Sections A and C of the first volume, and Part I, Section C, Part 2, Sections A, B and C, Part 3, Section B, and Sections A and B of Part 4 of *The reading curriculum* would probably be the most useful to the teacher of primary school children.

MOON, C. and RABAN, B. *A question of reading – organisation of resources for reading in primary schools* Ward Lock Educational, 1975. Chapters deal with the reading process, the needs and abilities of children, what books should provide for the reader (a particularly useful and insightful section of the book), the support materials available at the present time, the way in which children and reading materials can be matched, and practical advice on how to organise the reading class.

NEWTON, M. and THOMSON, M. E. *Dyslexia: a guide for teachers and parents*, Hodder and Stoughton, 1975. Written by the designers of the Aston Index (a measure for early detection of 'dyslexic' children) for those concerned with teaching the dyslexic – defined as someone who has difficulties of unstable perceptual patterns preventing the consistent learning of order and direction, which are involved in the sequential nature of written language. A short book which provides some insight into the very special difficulties that some children may experience in learning to read.

PETERS, M. L. *Diagnostic and remedial spelling manual* Macmillan Educational, 1975. Outlines the case for predictive and diagnostic testing in spelling, drawing upon the work of the psycholinguists, which suggests that some spelling 'mistakes' or approximations may be better than others and can be used to assess a child's grasp of spelling 'correctness'. Includes three continuous prose passages for dictation using words of different frequency in children's vocabulary, but the whole of this short book would be useful for the teacher considering children's spelling as part of free writing, news, etc.

ROSEN, H. ed. *Language and literacy in our schools – some appraisals of the Bullock Report* University of London Institute of Education, from NFER Publishing Company, 1975. The producers of this volume considered that the *Bullock Report* was impoverished by its lack of documentation, especially in regard to using and quoting from children's own language. The contributors draw upon this type of material with Margaret Spenser and Moira McKenzie writing on 'Learning to read and the reading process', John Dixon on 'Talk and collaborative learning', and Josie Levive and Alex McLeod on 'Children from families of overseas origins'.

SCHONELL, F. J. and GOODACRE, E. J. *The psychology and teaching of reading* Oliver and Boyd, 5th edn 1974. Chs 3–8 particularly relevant for the teacher in the primary school; appendix includes lists of materials, language development programmes, etc.

STOTT, D. H. *The parent as teacher* Hodder and Stoughton, 1974. Describes games and materials which teach children how to use their minds, develop patience, and learn how to learn. Provides information for parents and teachers as to how to help apparently retarded children to develop their abilities and includes a chapter on the development of reading skills.

TAYLOR, J. *Reading and writing in the first school* Allen and Unwin, 1973. Deals with the factors involved in reading, approaches, methods, different media; includes chapters on phonics and linguistics, learning to write, classroom organisation for pre-readers, beginners, advancing and fluent readers.

TROWBRIDGE, N. E. *The new media challenge* (a language project language guide), Macmillan Educational, 1974. Clearly outlines a wide range of audio visual aids and their uses, some of which can be related to the teaching of reading. Includes information about the use of tape recorders, the development of listening skills, reading programmes on radio and television, uses for magnet boards, and the *Language master* and the *Audio-page*. Contains a number of clear drawings which provide useful details.

WALKER, C. *Reading development and extension* Ward Lock Educational, 1974. Mainly intended for the junior and secondary teacher but includes useful information on planning a programme for developing reading skills and fostering enjoyment of reading, e.g. explanation of SQ3R technique and the development of reading comprehension through prediction and deletion exercises, the use of reading laboratories (graded boxed reading materials) and the individual reading interview.

WALKER, C. *Teaching pre-reading skills* Ward Lock Educational, 1975. Details of materials, techniques and forms of organisation to help the development of pre-reading skills in the areas of visual and auditory discrimination and language development, including a chapter on 'teaching the letters'. Final chapter on recording and guiding progress includes details of Thackray reading readiness profiles and the use for assessment purposes of Stott's 'Flying Start' material.

WILKINSON, A. M. *The foundations of language: talking and reading in young children,* Oxford University Press, 1971. Begins with an account of modern linguistic theory, paying special attention to the non-linguistic context of speech and then describing the way in which children acquire language and how this relates to thinking. Concludes with a section on reading describing various methods and approaches in the main suggested by eminent linguists.

Appendix 2 List of Publishers' addresses

ABBATT, P. & M., 29 Marylebone Road, London W1.

ABELARD-SCHUMAN LTD., 450 Edgware Road, London W2 1EG.

ALEXANDER, GEORGE PHILIP, Norfolk House, Smallbrook, Queensway, Birmingham.

ALPHA EDUCATIONAL, Hook Road, Kingsclere, Nr Newbury, Berks.

ARNOLD, E. J. & SON LTD., Butterley Street, Leeds LS10 1AX.

ARNOLD, EDWARD (PUBLISHERS) LTD., Woodlands Park Avenue, Maidenhead, Berks.

ATHENA REPRODUCTIONS, Bishops Stortford, Herts.

AUTOBATES LEARNING SYSTEMS LTD., Whitestone House, Lutterworth Road, Nuneaton.

BBC PUBLICATIONS, 35 Marylebone High Street, London W1M 4AA.

BELL & HOWELL, Alperton House, Bridgewater Road, Wembley, Middx.

BENN, ERNEST LTD., Sovereign Way, Tonbridge, Kent.

BETTER BOOKS, 11 Springfield Place, Lansdown Road, Bath BA1 5RA.

BLACK, A. & C., 4 Soho Square, London W1V 6AD.

BLACKIE & SON LTD., Bishopbriggs, Glasgow, G64 2NZ. (London Office: 5 Fitzhardinge Street, London W1.)

BLACKWELL, BASIL, 49 Broad Street, Oxford.

BLOND EDUCATIONAL, Iliffe House, Iliffe Avenue, Oadby, Leics.

BODLEY HEAD LTD., 9 Bow Street, Covent Garden, London WC2 7AL.

BROCKHAMPTON PRESS LTD., Salisbury Road, Leicester. (Now Hodder & Stoughton Children's Books)

BROTHER OFFICE EQUIPMENT, 964 High Road, Finchley, London.

BURKE PUBLISHING CO. LTD., 14 John Street, London WC1N 2EJ.

BUTTERWORTH & CO., 88 Kingsway, London WC2.

CAMBRIDGE UNIVERSITY PRESS, PO Box 92, London NW1 2DB.

CAPE, JONATHAN LTD., 30 Bedford Square, London, WC1.

CASSELL & COLLIER-MACMILLAN LTD., 35 Red Lion Square, London WC1R 4SG.

CHAMBERS, W. & R., 11 Thistle Street, Edinburgh EH2 1DG.

CHAPMAN, GEOFFREY (A division of Cassell & Collier-Macmillan).

CHARLES & SON LTD. (Grant Educational) 91/95 Union Street, Glasgow.

CHATTO & WINDUS LTD., 40/42 William IV Street, London WC2E 9BR.

CI AUDIO VISUAL LTD., Durham Road, Borehamwood, Herts.

COLLINS, WILLIAM SONS & CO. LTD., 144 Cathedral Street, Glasgow, G4 0NB.

COMMON GROUND FILMSTRIPS, Longman Group Ltd., Pinnacles, Harlow.

CUISENAIRE CO. LTD., 40 Silver Street, Reading.

C-Z SCIENTIFIC INSTRUMENTS LTD., 93/97 New Cavendish Street, London W1A 2AR.

DALGLIESH HAYWARD & ASSOCIATES LTD., 196 Fernbank Road, Ascot, Berks.

DAVIS & MOUGHTON LTD., Ludgate House, 23 Waterloo Place, Leamington Spa, Warwicks.

DENT, J. M. & SONS LTD., 10 Bedford Street, London, WC2E 9RB.

DEUTSCH, ANDRE LTD., 105 Great Russell Street, London WC1B 3LJ.

DINOSAUR PUBLICATIONS, Beechcroft, Fen End, Over, Cambridge.

DRAKE EDUCATIONAL ASSOCIATES LTD., 212 Whitchurch Road, Cardiff.

EARLY LEARNING CENTRE, 173 King's Road, Reading.

EDUCATIONAL EVALUATION ENTERPRISES, Queen Anne House, Queen Square, Bristol.

EDUCATIONAL PRODUCTIONS LTD, Bradford Road, East Ardsley, Wakefield, Yorks.

ENCYCLOPAEDIA BRITANNICA, Dorland House, 18 Regent Street, London W1.

ESA CREATIVE LEARNING LTD., PO Box 22, Pinnacles, Harlow, Essex.

EVANS BROTHERS LTD., Montague House, Russell Square, London WC1.

FIELD ENTERPRISE EDUCATIONAL CORPORATION, Canterbury House, Sydenham Road, Croydon.

GALLERY FIVE, 14 Ogle Street, London W1.

GALT, JAMES & CO. LTD., Brookfield Road, Cheadle, Cheshire.
  (Toys only from 30/31 Great Marlborough Street, London W1).

GATEWAY EDUCATIONAL MEDIA, St Lawrence House, 29/31 Broad Street, Bristol.

GIBSON, ROBERT & SONS LTD., 17 Fitzroy Place, Glasgow, G3.

GINN & CO. LTD., Elsinore House, Buckingham Street, Aylesbury, Bucks.

GOOD READING LTD., 27 Chancery Lane, London WC2.

GORDON FRASER BOOKS (Represented in Great Britain by Book Representation Ltd., 37 Stone Street, London WC1.)

THE GRAIL, 125 Waxwell Lane, Pinner, Middx.

GRANT EDUCATIONAL CO. LTD., 91 Union Street, Glasgow G1.

GREENWOOD, G., 67 Heath Farm, Norton, Stourbridge, Worcs.

HAMISH HAMILTON LTD., 90 Great Russell Street, London WC1 3PT.

HAMLYN GROUP, 42 The Centre, Feltham, Middx.

HARRAP, GEORGE G. & CO. LTD., PO Box 70, 182 High Holborn, London WC1.

HART-DAVIS EDUCATIONAL LTD., Frogmore, St. Albans, Herts.

HEINEMANN EDUCATIONAL, 48 Charles Street, Mayfair, W1X 8AH.

HERON BOOKS, 18 St. Anne's Crescent, London SW18.

HODDER & STOUGHTON, St. Paul's House, Warwick Lane, EC4.

HOLMES MCDOUGALL LTD., Allander House, 137/141 Leith Walk, Edinburgh EH6 8NS.

HOLT RINEHART & WINSTON (HOLT-BLOND LTD.), 120 Golden Lane, Barbican, London EC1.

HOPE, THOMAS LTD., St. Philip's Drive, Royston, Oldham, Lancs.

HULTON EDUCATIONAL PUBLICATIONS LTD., Raans Road, Amersham, Bucks.

HUTCHINSON EDUCATIONAL, Tiptree, Colchester, Essex.

INITIAL TEACHING PUBLISHING CO. LTD., 9 Southampton Place, WC1.

INITIAL TEACHING ALPHABET FOUNDATION, Alma House, 2a Alma Road, Reigate, Surrey.

INVICTA PLASTICS Ltd., Oadby, Leics.

JACARANDA PRESS Pty. Ltd., 122 Regents Park Road, London NW1.

JOHNSON & BACON (See Cassell Collier-Macmillan)

KAYE & WARD LTD., 21 New Bond Street, London EC2M 4NT.

LADYBIRD BOOKS LTD., P.O. Box 12, Beeches Road, Loughborough.

LEARNING DEVELOPMENT AIDS, Park Works, Norwich Road, Wisbech, Cambs.

LONGMAN GROUP LTD., Longman House, Burnt Mill, Harlow, Essex.

LUTTERWORTH PRESS, Luke House, Farnham Road, Guildford, Surrey.

MACDONALD EDUCATIONAL, Holywell House, Worship Street, London EC2.

MACMILLAN EDUCATION LTD., Houndmills, Basingstoke, Hants.

MAGIC STEPS PUBLICATIONS, 93 Victoria Road, Exmouth, Devon.

MATTHEWS, DREW & SHELBOURNE LTD., 78 High Holborn, London WC1.

3M CO. LTD., 3M House, Wigmore Street, London W1.

MCGRAW HILL CO. LTD., Shoppenhangers Road, Maidenhead, Berks.

METHUEN EDUCATIONAL, 11 New Fetter Lane, London EC4P 4EE.

MOOR PLATT PRESS, 294 Chorley New Road, Horwich, Lancs.

MULLER, FREDERICK LTD., Victoria Works, Edgware Road, London NW2

N.F.E.R., The Mere, Upton Park, Slough, Berks. or Test Division, 2 Jennings Buildings, Thames, Windsor.

NELSON, THOMAS & SONS LTD., 36 Park Street, London W1Y 4DE.

NEWNES, GEORGE, Hamlyn House, 42 The Centre, Feltham, Middx.

NISBET, JAMES & CO. LTD., Digswell Place, Welwyn, Herts.

OFFICE & ELECTRONIC MACHINES LTD., 140/154 Borough High Street, London SE1.

OLIVER & BOYD, Croythorn House, 23 Ravelston Terrace, Edinburgh EH4 3TJ.

OPEN UNIVERSITY, Walton Hall, Milton Keynes, Bucks.

OXFORD UNIVERSITY PRESS, Walton Street, Oxford.

PACE INTERNATIONAL LTD., Now c/o Holmes McDougall.

PACKMAN RESEARCH LTD., Twyford, Berks.

PAIGE FREIZES, The Manor House, Kings Cliffe, Peterborough.

PAN BOOKS LTD., Cavaye Place, London SW10 9PG.

PENGUIN EDUCATIONAL, Harmondsworth, Middlesex UB7 0DA.

PERGAMON PRESS LTD., Headington Hill Hall, Oxford.

PHILIP & TACEY LTD., North Way, Andover, Hants.

PICTOGRAM SUPPLIES, Barton, Cambridge.

PITMAN, SIR ISSAC & SONS LTD., 39 Parker Street, London WC2B 5PB.

PURNELL BANCROFT, 49/50 Poland Street, London W1A 2LG.

RANK AUDIO VISUAL, P.O. Box 60, Great West Road, Brentford, Middlesex.

READERS DIGEST, 25 Berkeley Square, London W1X 6AB.

RED CIRCLE TOYS LTD., Education Aids Division, PO Box 25, Winchester, Hants.

REEVES & DRYAD, (Four to Eight Ltd), Medway House, St Mary's Mills, Evelyn Drive, Leicester LE3 3BT.

REMEDIAL SUPPLY CO., Dixon Street, Wolverhampton, Staffs.

SCHOFIELD & SIMS LTD., 35 St John's Road, Huddersfield HD1 5DT.

SCHOLASTIC PUBLICATIONS LTD., 161 Fulham Road, London SW3 6SW.

SCIENCE RESEARCH ASSOCIATES, Newtown Road, Henley-on-Thames, Oxon.

SCOTT-FORESMAN & CO., 32 West Street, Brighton SM1 2RT.

SENLAC SYSTEMS, 351 Portobello Road, London W10.

SLIDE CENTRE LTD., Portman House, 17 Brodrick Street, London SW17.

SPCK BOOKSHOP LTD., Holy Trinity Church, Marylebone Road, London NW1 4DU.

SPECIAL EDUCATION PUBLICATIONS, Street Cottage, North Waltham, Basingstoke.

STILLITRON, 72 New Bond Street, London W1Y 0XY.

TASKMASTER LTD., Morris Road, Clarendon Park, Leicester.

THREE FOUR FIVE (Kiddicraft), 37 Great Russell Street, London WC1.

THURMAN PUBLISHING LTD., 24 Old Bond Street, London W1X 3DA.

TRANSATLANTIC PLASTICS LTD., Transatlantic Garden Estate, Ventnor, I.O.W.

TRANSWORLD PUBLISHERS LTD., Cavendish House, 57/59 Uxbridge Road, London W5.

TULL GRAPHIC LTD., 84 Teesdale Street, London E2.

ULVERSCROFT LARGE PRINT BOOKS LTD., Station Road, Glenfield, Leicester.

UNITS OF SOUND PRODUCTIONS, 23 Pool Green Neston, Corsham, Wilts., SN13 9SN.

UNIVERSITY OF LONDON PRESS, Saint Paul's House, Warwick Lane, London EC4 (now Hodder and Stoughton Educational).

WARD LOCK EDUCATIONAL, 116 Baker Street, London W1M 2BB.

WARNE, FREDERICK & CO. LTD., Chandos House, Bedford Court, London WC2.

WATTS, FRANKLIN LTD., 1 Vere Street, London, W1.

WESTON WOODS STUDIOS LTD., P.O. Box 2, Henley-on-Thames, Oxon.

WHEATON, A. & C., Hennock Road, Exeter, EX2 8RP.

WOODFORD EDUCATIONAL PUBLICATIONS, 178 Snakes Lane, Woodford Green, Essex.

WORLD BOOK ENCYCLOPAEDIA, Canterbury House, Sydenham Road, Croydon.

WORLD'S WORK LTD., The Windmill Press, Kingswood, Tadworth, Surrey.

YOUNG WORLD PRODUCTIONS, Young World House, 550b London Road, North Cheam, Surrey (Now part of Nelson).

Index